ENGLISH

Louise Moore

RISING★STARS

Rising Stars UK Ltd, 7 Hatchers Mews, Bermondsey Street,
London SE1 3GS
www.risingstars-uk.com

Published 2013

Project Manager and Editorial: Dawn Booth
Design: Words & Pictures Ltd, London
Cover Design: Words & Pictures Ltd, London

British Library Cataloguing-in-Publication Data.
A CIP record for this book is available from the British Library.

ISBN: 978-0-85769-637-3
Printed by Ashford Colour Press Ltd
Acknowledgement: p.64 photo iStock/Heidi Van der Westhuizen

Contents

How to use this book

The books in this series have been written to support teachers preparing pupils for the Level 6 tests at the end of Key Stage 2. This is a difficult level to achieve, and teachers should ensure that pupils have reached a high Level 5 and have the necessary maturity to tackle higher-level work.

Each section is presented as a two-page spread, one page for the teacher and the other for the pupil. The layout of these pages is explained below.

(1) Each 'Teacher overview' page starts by identifying the key points, which are the essential teaching points that need to be communicated to the pupils.

(2) The 'Teacher overview' page contains the main information about each topic, covering the rules and principles. Where relevant, worked examples are shown.

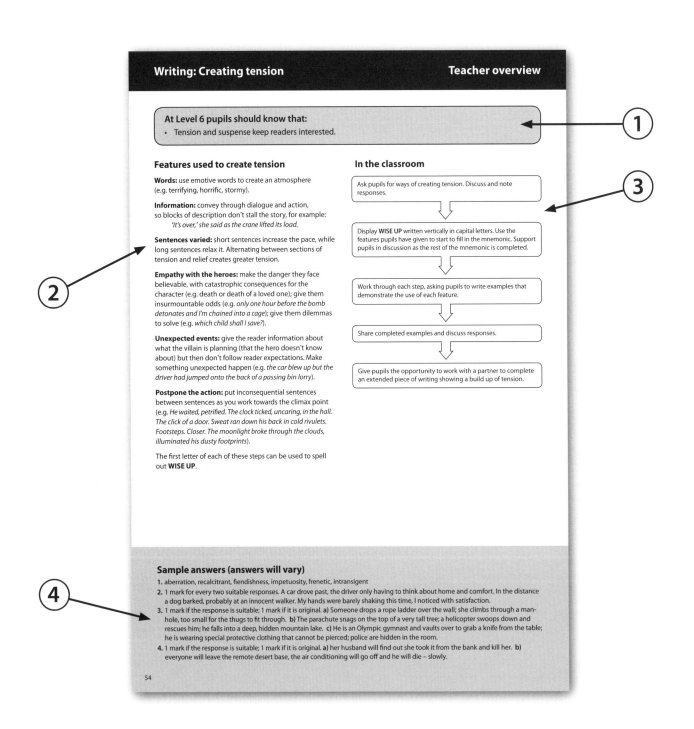

(3) Possible teaching steps, in the 'In the classroom' section, suggest ways that the topic could be introduced to pupils, often building on Level 5 knowledge. These need to be read before the lesson as some preparation may be necessary.

(4) Answers are included on the 'Teacher overview' page for quick and easy reference in the lesson. Where relevant, there is guidance for allocation of marks.

(5) The 'Pupil task' worksheets are photocopiable.

(6) Each worksheet starts with easier, more straightforward questions.

(7) The questions progressively become harder.

(8) Marks for each question are shown to guide pupils as to the complexity of the answer required.

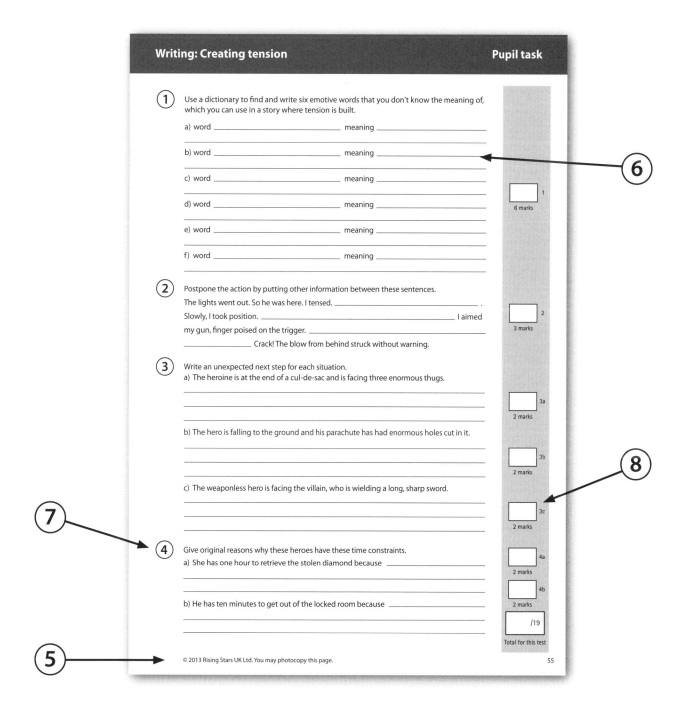

Writing: Creating tension — **Pupil task**

1. Use a dictionary to find and write six emotive words that you don't know the meaning of, which you can use in a story where tension is built.

   a) word _____ meaning _____

   b) word _____ meaning _____

   c) word _____ meaning _____

   d) word _____ meaning _____

   e) word _____ meaning _____

   f) word _____ meaning _____

   [1] 6 marks

2. Postpone the action by putting other information between these sentences.
   The lights went out. So he was here. I tensed. _____ .
   Slowly, I took position. _____ I aimed
   my gun, finger poised on the trigger. _____
   _____ Crack! The blow from behind struck without warning.

   [2] 3 marks

3. Write an unexpected next step for each situation.
   a) The heroine is at the end of a cul-de-sac and is facing three enormous thugs.
   _____
   _____
   _____

   [3a] 2 marks

   b) The hero is falling to the ground and his parachute has had enormous holes cut in it.
   _____
   _____
   _____

   [3b] 2 marks

   c) The weaponless hero is facing the villain, who is wielding a long, sharp sword.
   _____
   _____
   _____

   [3c] 2 marks

4. Give original reasons why these heroes have these time constraints.
   a) She has one hour to retrieve the stolen diamond because _____
   _____
   _____

   [4a] 2 marks

   b) He has ten minutes to get out of the locked room because _____
   _____
   _____

   [4b] 2 marks

   /19
   Total for this test

55

5

Important guidance for KS2 teachers

Achieving a Level 6 in English is a very different proposition to achieving a Level 6 in maths, where the focus is on learning new facts and skills and then applying them to more complex problems which have an absolute right or wrong answer. If you intend to give pupils the opportunity to achieve Level 6 English, then it is important that you prepare them well and that they understand the demands and complexities of work at Level 6.

Below are some points that need to be considered.

Pupil maturity

In responding to questions about the intention of the writer and reason why different techniques are used, the pupils need the emotional maturity to understand motives and the language skills to express these in a clear and concise way. These are skills that are linked to pupil experience and maturity. Some pupils may be gifted in the use of language but not yet have the maturity to tackle some of the higher-level questions.

Higher-level thinking skills

Much of the English reading paper requires not only the use of higher-level thinking skills, but also the ability to use them quickly. In the test situation, pupils have a limited amount of time to read and respond to questions that demand higher-level thinking skills. Some pupils who are capable of working at Level 6 can fail to achieve the level in the test because they have not yet developed the necessary speed for processing their thoughts and recording their ideas succinctly on paper.

The importance of discussion and debate

Pupils who could possibly achieve Level 6 require extra time to provide for their special needs. In English, particularly, much of the work needs to be exploratory, with lots of time to discuss ideas and alternatives. Everybody has different ideas and, whilst all points of view may be valid, these must be supported by reasoned argument and explanation. Within each topic, the possible teaching steps suggested in this book require time for discussion between pupils and as a group led by the teacher. This is an essential element of giving pupils the opportunity to reach those higher levels. If there is only one pupil working at this level, then a lot of one-to-one time will be necessary.

Creating a climate for success

Pupils exploring Level 6 work may be academically talented, but this does not mean that they are necessarily confident – especially in their ability to succeed with the more demanding work. Pupils need to be set up for success each step of the way, including understanding that making mistakes and finding some concepts more difficult is a natural part of the learning journey. Just as other pupils are given support to achieve their potential at lower levels, so must pupils working towards Level 6.

Question types on the reading paper

Nearly all the questions on the reading paper involve pupils explaining how or why features are used and the effect they have, or giving and justifying opinions. Pupils need plenty of practice in responding to these questions from a wide variety of texts. At least in the initial stages, much of this work needs to be done orally, with discussion about the merits of different responses.

Using the text in the reading test

One of the key skills that pupils must master is using the text in responding to questions. Referring to the content and purpose of each particular text and using quotes to support answers is an essential element of achieving a Level 6 in English. Pupils should supply the answer, back it up with textual evidence and then explain how the evidence supports the point they are making. Incorporating this into all discussions and reading work is absolutely vital – pupils need to reach a stage where they are doing this automatically. General responses that could equally apply to a different text are not sufficient.

Provision of dedicated time for Level 6 pupils

If you have pupils working towards Level 6, then ideally they will be on a special education plan (even if it is just in your own thinking and planning) and will be receiving some dedicated time each week. If there is no provision for this, then talk to colleagues about how it might be achieved. If your class is taught by another adult at any time in the week (such as a specialist teacher or sports coach), it may occasionally be possible to give the Level 6 pupils some dedicated time then.

Catering for Level 6 pupils in class lessons

The majority of the pupil time will, nevertheless, be spent in class. While some class work (such as writing) is equally valid whatever the pupil level, and other elements can be used as revision (such as types of figurative language and punctuation) there will be times when the general class work is not suitable for Level 6 pupils and extension or alternative work will have to be provided. Remember to treat them as another group in the class, who still need their share of teaching and support if they are to make progress, and incorporate this into your planning so they get their fair share of your time over a week.

Suggested answers in these books

A lot of literacy questions have more than one possible answer and most answers can be worded in more than one way. When marking pupil work, discretion needs to be used in deciding whether the question has been answered, but sample answers are provided for most questions to give some guidance in what would constitute an acceptable answer.

Reading assessment

Photocopy the reading text so it is doubled-sided on a sheet of A4 and the paper can then be folded to make a booklet to be used along with the answer sheets in the assessment.

At Level 6 pupils should be able to:

- Explain the writer's purpose and views, using words and quotations from the text to support their ideas.

At Level 6 reading pupils must be able to use quotes from the text to support their answers. Quickly locating the information that is needed is an important skill.

Ensure that your pupils know what a quotation is – they need to copy the word(s) exactly from the text and put inverted commas around the copied word or phrase. It should not be written in their own words. For example:

Alex walked reluctantly towards the sea.

Question: How does the author show that Alex didn't want to go near the sea?

Answer: He says that he 'walked reluctantly' which means that he wasn't keen to go.

I quivered as I entered the room. Keeping myself firmly in check, I looked at the faces turned towards me and gave stare for stare till they looked away.

Question: How does the author show that he is in control of the situation? Use quotation to support your answer.

Answer: He says that he holds himself 'firmly in check' showing he is in control, and that he out-stared the people because 'they looked away', meaning he was stronger.

The selected quotation must support the answer being given to the question. It should give evidence that backs up their viewpoint or explanation. If possible, pupils should find more than one quotation to support their view.

Writing the quotation within their sentence is a skill that needs to be practised.

In the classroom

Select a text for the pupils to use.

Ask pupils to locate and point to sentences that illustrate a given point. Start with easier examples and gradually make them more complex, where information has to be deduced from the text.

Ask pupils to work in pairs to formulate sentences that explain what their quotation shows and how it shows this.

Once pupils are quick and adept at this exercise, have them write their answers, emphasising the need to be clear and concise.

Move pupils on to independent work. At Level 6 they should be able to find a suitable quotation (or two) and explain what that quotation does to show the author's intentions.

Answers

Up to 2 marks for the quotations and 1 mark for a suitable explanation.
1. a) 'day was over', 'flickering candlelight':
2. a) 'hurried movements', 'hissed orders'   b) 'thrilled to reach the hut', 'carefree laugh'
3. a) 'like a bullet', 'it stopped my heart'   b) 'had to get through', 'Now', 'Nothing was going to stop me'

1

> Once the day was over, Jake felt drained. He looked wearily at the box, knowing that he had to deal with it before he could have his long overdue rest. His muscles screamed as he bent to examine the lock in the flickering candlelight.

How does the writer show that it is dark? Support your answer with quotations from the paragraph.

_____

_____

_____

1

3 marks

2

> Bounding over the hills like a gazelle, Jo was thrilled to reach the hut in a bare hour. Her early arrival caused consternation. Hurried movements and hissed orders could be heard before she even lifted the latch. With a carefree laugh, she burst in.

a) How does the writer show that the occupants of the hut were trying to keep something secret from Jo? Support your answer with quotations from the paragraph.

_____

_____

_____

2a

3 marks

b) How does the writer show that Jo is not worried about anything that might be in the hut? Support your answer with quotations from the paragraph.

_____

_____

_____

2b

3 marks

3

> 'Don't!' The shout was like a bullet from a gun and it stopped my heart. It started again, beating even more furiously than before. I had to get through that door. Now. My breath came in painful gasps. I risked a quick glance over my shoulder before I charged the door with a hard straight battering ram. Nothing was going to stop me.

a) How does the writer show that the shout shocked him? Support your answer with quotations from the paragraph.

_____

_____

_____

3a

3 marks

b) How does the writer show that he wants to get through the door urgently? Support your answer with quotations from the paragraph.

_____

_____

_____

3b

3 marks

/15

Total for this test

> **At Level 6 pupils should know that:**
> - Information should support the point being made.
> - Information from more than one source gives even more support to a view.

Using more than one source

An argument, opinion or viewpoint is strengthened if evidence to support it can be found in more than one source. Evidence from two or more sources has a greater impact, as one text may be biased towards a particular standpoint. The more texts that can be used, the more convincing the argument will be.

Consider medical recommendations that are based on one piece of study and research; the medical profession would be very wary in acting upon these findings before they were verified in numerous other studies and tested in a variety of conditions. The more evidence there is, the more a 'truth' is likely to be accepted.

Using more than one source

It is important that quotes are used to back up assertions and these should be correctly punctuated (see the section in this book on 'Using quotations', pages 8–9).

Sample answers (answers will vary)

1. a) Dear Diary
   b) 1 mark for difference, 1 mark for at least two direct quotes. Dear Diary is negative ('At last, we're home', 'too hot', 'not a good idea', 'crowded', 'dangerous') while the other two are positive (Holiday Paradise: 'perfect', 'stunning', something for everyone', 'love', 'incredible', 'enjoy'; Athletics' Rising Star: 'opportunities', 'relaxation', 'inspiring', 'awe-inspiring', 'fascinating').
2. 1 mark for valid view, 1 mark for at least two direct quotes, 1 mark for supporting explanation.
   a) Good – 'winding roads and speedy descents', 'inspiring climbs and ancient routes' even though Dear Diary said the hills were 'massive' and it was 'too hot'.
   b) Interesting – 'historic', 'tiny streets', 'fascinating old towns had cool plazas'.
   c) Exciting – 'activities from diving to surfing', 'a warm sea for aquatic adventures' and only one text said that they were 'crowded'.

In the classroom

Activity 1

Give pupils short booklets that contain several short factual texts (old SAT papers are ideal – preferably, but not necessarily, at Level 6 – and can be found on the Internet if your school doesn't have any).

Ask pupils to look through the first article and either:
    a) list important views, ideas and beliefs.
or b) find evidence that supports or contradicts a viewpoint which you supply.

Compare and discuss responses.

Tell pupils to look through the second article and find evidence that supports or contradicts the evidence from the first article.

Continue with the other articles in the booklet.

Discuss findings and ask pupils to write a few sentences supporting or refuting the initial viewpoint, using the evidence they have gathered. Remind them how to punctuate quotations.

Activity 2

Look at two or three texts and list similarities and differences.

Working with a partner, allow pupils time to discuss and formulate questions that could be answered using the information from both or all of the texts.

Each pair should attempt to answer the questions formulated by other pupils.

1 Read the following texts and then answer the questions below.

Holiday Paradise	Dear Diary,	**Athletics' Rising Star**
Mallorca is a perfect holiday destination. With its sunny climate, stunning beaches and historic towns there is something for everyone: cyclists love the winding roads and speedy descents; climbers are challenged by incredible cliff faces; water enthusiasts enjoy activities from diving to surfing. Come and enjoy adventure and fun in the sun!	At last, we're home from Mallorca. It was really too hot to do anything, and being made to bike up all those massive hills was not a good idea. The beaches were crowded with silly little kids and the old towns, with tiny streets were, frankly, too dangerous to drive through – especially considering how Dad drives! They weren't even safe for walking. It's good to be home.	A few days in Mallorca revealed a plethora of opportunities for training and relaxation. There were cycle rides with inspiring climbs and ancient routes (try the old Pilgrims' Way if you feel adventurous), climbing in awe-inspiring scenery and a warm sea for aquatic adventures. Fascinating old towns had cool plazas to while away the evening and watch the world go by over a glass of the local brew.

a) Which text has a different opinion to the other two? _____

                                       1a   1 mark

b) How is it different? Support your answer with references to the texts.

_____

_____

_____

                                        1b   3 marks

2 Give an opinion on these topics, using evidence from all three texts to support your views:

a) cycling in Mallorca

_____

_____

_____

_____

                                        2a   3 marks

b) old towns in Mallorca

_____

_____

_____

_____

                                        2b   3 marks

c) the beaches and water sports in Mallorca

_____

_____

_____

_____

                                        2c   3 marks

                                        /13   Total for this test

> **At Level 6 pupils should be able to:**
> - Scan texts closely for specific information.
> - Identify main sentences in each paragraph.
> - Support answers by textual reference.

Finding specific information

By Level 6, a scan of the text should be sufficient to locate specific information to answer a question or support a point of view. By identifying key words and possible synonyms, a reader can conduct a search that is efficient both in time and in gathering the required material. More than one piece of information will probably be requested and some comment on similarities and differences between the pieces of information may be necessary.

Main sentences

Each section of a piece of writing has a purpose and this is conveyed in the main (or topic) sentence. Usually, this sentence is the first in the section, but the writer may place it elsewhere to create a different effect. For example, it could build suspense or create a greater impact to place the sentence at the end of the section, or placing it in the middle of the section can allow the writer to build information towards the main idea and then add further information to clarify after the topic sentence.

Using textual reference

This is a key skill at Level 6. Supporting answers using textual reference and direct quotes should be routine for pupils.

In the classroom

Activity 1

> Give pupils an unfamiliar text and have them find and point out specified pieces of information as quickly as possible.

> Ask pupils to use the text they find to formulate responses to related questions. Emphasise the need to use the text in the answer.

Activity 2

> Challenge pupils to scan a text and present the information as a short list.

> Compare answers and discuss.

Activity 3

> Ask pupils to highlight the main sentence in each paragraph of a text.

Sample answers (answers will vary)

1. **a)** tall, strong, dark **b)** fastest selling, top sellers, popular, most, greatest **c)** afternoon, later, before tea, after lunch **d)** shivered, pale, scared, anxious, worried, frown, tears, cringe **e)** got there, after, before, during

2. **a)** Years ago, people feared the flashing of cats' eyes at night. **b)** The Olympic Games were beginning. **c)** Some cartoons can deliver important messages.

3. 1 mark for each difference, up to 2 marks for the writer's preference.
   Canet: 'small', 'peaceful', 'sleepy', 'winding narrow streets', 'historic'; Parmes: 'bustling', 'noisy', 'fretful', 'stressed', 'straight boulevards', 'modern'; prefers Canet (Canet – 'beauty', 'breathtaking', 'interest', 'discerning visitor'; Parmes – 'crammed', 'fretful', 'slouching', 'stressed', 'no authentic character', 'not a must-see')

1 List words that you might scan a text for to find answers to these questions:

a) Describe the appearance of the man.

_____

b) Which items were the best sellers at the store?

_____

c) How did they spend the afternoon?

_____

d) How does the writer show the boy was afraid?

_____

e) When did they arrive at the hotel?

_____

1 | 5 marks

2 Underline the main sentence in each of these paragraphs.

a) Years ago, people feared the flashing of cats' eyes at night. They believed the light was proof of evil spirits, causing the eyes to project light. Actually, cats' eyes don't reflect light. They only seem to glow.

b) The occasion was historic. The preparation had taken years: training had been rigorous and unremitting. A nation watched anxiously and expectantly. The Olympic Games were beginning.

c) Cartoons – which is your favourite? It might be a show on television, or a comic strip in a magazine or paper. Cartoons can make you laugh but this is not always the aim of all cartoons. Some cartoons can deliver important messages. Using characters, the artist can make readers aware of political problems, social injustices and important events that could affect the future. There is often a serious truth behind the humour.

2 | 3 marks

3 Read the following passages and then answer the question.

> Canet is a small, peaceful town in the foothills of the mountains. Winding narrow streets of historic buildings may make driving hazardous, but they have a beauty all of their own. Hidden pathways, sleepy plazas and breathtaking views ensure there is always something to interest the more discerning visitor.
>
> Parmes is a town on the plains by the sea. Bustling beaches, crammed with fretful toddlers, slouching teenagers and stressed parents, are approached along straight, open boulevards. The demolition necessary to create these streets has meant that bright, modern shopping arenas, where authentic character is not a detail that worried the designer, have had the space to spring into life. This is not a must-see for the traveller with taste.

3 | 6 marks

Describe two differences between the towns and explain why the writer prefers one of them.

_____

_____

_____

_____

_____

/14

Total for this test

> **At Level 6 pupils should know that:**
> - The main message of the text should be summarised in a few sentences, a few words or even in one word.
> - Information from more than one place in the text should be used to support answers.

Summarising the text

Texts can be summarised in several ways:

   a. as a few sentences
   b. as one sentence
   c. as a key word
   d. as a list of important points
   e. as an information web
   f. in a chart, table or diagram
   g. for descriptions, by drawing a picture or map.

Whatever method is used, the key message of the text should still be evident. Diagrams and charts allow supporting evidence to be captured, while succinct methods ensure that the main message is the focus of the reading. Exploring the relevance and form of the title also helps pupils to understand the purpose of the text. Methods d, e and f (above) are like doing a plan for the writing after it has been completed.

Using information from more than one place in the text

After reading a text, there should be an awareness of how different parts of the text work together and how they give evidence that support views and statements. In answering questions, presenting information from different sections of the text creates a stronger platform to support points that are being made.

In the classroom

Activity 1

Ask pupils to scan a text, listing the points they think are important. Compare and discuss answers.

In pairs, tell pupils to sequence the points from most to least important. Compare answers and discuss.

Ask pupils to summarise the text in two sentences, then do so again in a few words and then select a key word. Examine and discuss the summaries.

Use the key words to evaluate the title and decide how appropriate it is. Challenge pupils to create an alternative title.

Activity 2

Ask pupils to use different colours to mark facts and opinions in a piece of writing.

Establish whether fact or opinion is prevalent and discuss why this might be the case for this particular piece of text (what is the genre, the purpose and the audience?).

Sample answers (answers will vary)

1. a) Learning to play an instrument is difficult in many ways.
   b) I cope with pressure by eating a lot.
   c) Thank you (but not much) for the scarf.
2. a) 1 mark for the main point from each paragraph.
   the plague came to Eyam in 1665; it came in some cloth; villagers stayed in the village; many families lost lots of members; the plague lasted a year.
   b) 1 mark for fair attempt, 2 marks for fuller answer.
   Villagers in Eyam were brave in dealing with an outbreak of the plague.

1 Write one sentence to summarise the information in these texts.

a) Learning to play an instrument is not a simple matter. There is the time needed to attend lessons and practise the skills and knowledge that are taught. There is the difficulty of training muscles to move and create sounds in ways that do not feel entirely comfortable. There is the cost of the instrument (unless you are a singer), the accessories and the lessons. It is not a task to be undertaken lightly.

_____

b) When I feel under pressure I have my own ways of coping. Some people get stressed and angry, venting their frustration on anyone unwary enough to cross their path. Others cope by going into a shell and refusing to emerge until the situation improves. I don't do either of those. I eat. Anything edible in the house is in danger of disappearing into the bottomless cavern that is my response to problems.

_____

c) Dear Max,
Thank you for your parcel. I loved the present you sent for Christmas. I know my friends will be really envious of the scarf with the little blue bunnies on the end. I was going to wear it when I went with the gang to the football match on Saturday but didn't want to get it dirty. Mum made me put it on but I thoughtfully hid it under the hedge as soon as I left the house. I hope you like the pink mittens I sent for you.
From Isidore

_____

	1
3 marks	

2 a) Find the main points in this text and list them in order of importance.

Eyam, in Derbyshire, suffered a terrible blow in 1665. In August, George Vicars, the village tailor, received some cloth that contained plague-infested fleas. He died a few days later and the plague took hold in the village.

After some debate, the villagers agreed to stay within the village to stop the spread of the disease through the surrounding countryside. Food and supplies were left at village boundaries and were paid for by coins left in wells and stone indents filled with vinegar to help prevent spreading infection.

Church services were held outdoors to reduce the spread of infection but many villagers were still killed by the disease. Some families lost many members: six of the Sydall family died; Elizabeth Hancock buried her husband and six children within one week.

The plague ravaged the village for over a year and over 260 villagers died. Their courage saved many other villages from a similar fate and is remembered to this day.

_____

_____

_____

_____

	2a
4 marks	

b) Write one sentence to summarise the text.

_____

	2b
2 marks	

	/9
Total for this test	

> **At Level 6 pupils should know that:**
> - Different readers may interpret the same text in different ways.
> - Inference is what is implied by the text as well as what is literally stated.

Inference

Inference means taking the information you are given and using it to deduce other facts about what you are reading. The deduced information is implied rather than stated. Clues can be scattered around the text so finding them and piecing them together is rather like doing a puzzle or acting as a detective. Answers should always be supported by evidence from the text. Elements that can support inference are:

- word order
- empathy with the characters
- actions of characters
- dialogue
- context of the words
- prior knowledge and experiences
- character emotion
- author's intent
- understanding of motive and intent.

It is important that quotes are used to back up assertions in the answers and these should be correctly punctuated (see the section in this book on 'Using quotations', pages 8–9).

Knowledge about where, when, how, what and why can be deduced from texts, depending on the information given. What can be inferred depends upon the understanding of the readers. This may relate to their reading ability in terms of decoding words, the accessibility of the text in terms of comprehension, or the previous experience and maturity of the reader (including culture norms and expectations). For example:

> *There was a small wooden stick in the middle of a sticky patch on the path.*

We could infer that there was an ice-lolly, that it had been dropped and that it melted.

In the classroom

> Tell pupils they are going to try to disguise some information without actually telling any untruths. Describe a scenario where, after a game during a wet playtime, a group of children in a classroom have broken a window when throwing something around the room.

> Ask pupils to work in pairs to discuss and formulate statements about the classroom that will imply that all is not well, without stating what has happened. For example:
>
> *Although the doors and windows were fastened there was a wet patch on the carpet where the rain was coming in. There was a toy car on the grass outside the classroom, despite the fact that nobody had been allowed outdoors. The children sat quietly in their places, casting apprehensive glances at the door, waiting for their teacher to return.*

> Collect and discuss responses, compiling the most effective sentences into a paragraph.

Sample answers (answers will vary)

1. 1 mark for one piece of information, 2 marks for more. **a)** it was winter, cold, night-time **b)** at the beach, built a sand-castle, tide coming in **c)** at the dentist, got toothache, afraid **d)** in trouble, expecting punishment, Tom could be poor (no shoes)
2. **a)** oblivious to the time, scents that tingled all his senses, twitched his nose, loping bound, followed the pack, join the hunt that would provide food for them all **b)** wolf (good sense of smell, moves with a bound, obeys the leader, hunts in a pack)
3. **a)** New Year / end of war / festival day **b)** start of war **c)** an alarm / invasion
4. **a)** dawn / early morning (grey light fragmented the blackness, dew – the wet grass) **b)** running away / thrown out / forced to leave / companion died (slipping out, heavy bag, tears, trudge determinedly)

1 Give at least two pieces of information that can be inferred from these pieces of text.

a) I buttoned up my coat and collected a torch before venturing into the back garden.

_____

b) She watched sadly as the castle she had laboured over washed silently away.

_____

c) I sat apprehensively in the waiting room, touching the painful area with my tongue. Perhaps I should just go home and take a pain-killer.

_____

d) With ragged trousers, bare feet and a smudge on his nose, Tom waited submissively for whatever consequences there would be.

_____

	1

8 marks

2 a) Underline the evidence in this text that suggests Jack is not a human.

> Jack rolled over, oblivious to the time or anything apart from the warmth of the sun on his back. He stretched, sniffing the early autumn scents that tingled all his senses and twitched his nose in appreciation. With a loping bound, he followed the pack, summoned by the leader's call to join the hunt that would provide food for them all.

b) What type of animal do you think Jack is? Support your answer with evidence from the text.

_____

_____

_____

	2

2 marks

3 Give possible events for these happenings, using the text to support your answers.

a) At midnight, the bells pealed out across the town. People began to cheer.

_____

b) At midnight, the bells pealed out across the town. People looked at each other in weary resignation or hopeful expectation, depending on their understanding of the event.

_____

c) At midnight, the bells pealed out across the town. People emerged into the streets in sleepy confusion.

_____

	3

3 marks

4 Read the passage, then answer the questions using the text to support your answers.

> Slipping out of the house as grey light fragmented the blackness of the surrounding trees, Joshua shouldered his heavy bag. Tears ran unnoticed over his sunken cheeks as, without a backward glance, he started to trudge determinedly towards the track, leaving heavy footprints in the wet grass – footprints that would fade when the sun cast a gaze over them.

a) What is the time of day? _____

b) Why do you think Joshua was leaving? _____

_____

	4

4 marks

	/17

Total for this test

> **At Level 6 pupils should know that:**
> - Some of the key purposes of a text are to explain, instruct, persuade, inform and entertain.
> - The purpose of a text can be established through its layout, language and key words.

Explanations of purposes

Explanation: tells how or why something works or happened.

Instruction: gives a series of steps on how to do something.

Persuasion: presents arguments and opinions to influence the reader's viewpoint.

Information: gives facts to improve understanding.

Entertainment: for recreation and enjoyment.

Questions related to text purpose

Questions tend to ask directly what the purpose of the text is, or why the author wrote it.

Answering questions about text purpose

It is not sufficient to answer this type of question with general answers such as 'to persuade the reader'. The answer requires an explanation of the text purpose as it relates to the particular text and examples from the text that illustrate the points made in the answer. Consider:

What is the purpose of the text on this page?

Answer: The purpose of the text is to inform teachers about possible different purposes of a text, shown by the heading 'Explanations of purposes'. Another purpose is to provide instructions on teaching – the points in 'In the classroom' – that teachers may wish to use. A further purpose is to explain how pupils should approach answering questions about text purpose, telling them to 'relate it to the particular text'.

In the classroom

Show pupils examples of different types of text (use short articles where possible) and ask them to discuss with a partner why they think each text was written.

Collect responses and discuss why they chose the purposes they did. Emphasise that their answers should refer back to the text (to persuade the reader to …, to inform the reader about …, to explain why …).

Display all the purposes given and ask pupils to work with their partner to put the different purposes into groups which have a similar purpose.

Collect and compare responses and agree together the main group headings

For one group, work together to write aspects of the text that show it belongs to that group (emphasise layout, language style and key words).

Ask pupils to do the same with each of the other groups.

---

1 Write the type of text in the group that reflects its main purpose for each of the following:

a joke book, electricity bill, directions to Bugsworth Basin, advert, a DIY manual, junk mail, encyclopaedia, leaflet on how to operate your phone, short story, label on a medicine bottle, a letter answering a complaint, charity leaflet, telephone directory, 'How televisions work' book, a book about the Indian landscape, leaflet from a political party

Explanation	Information	Persuasion
Instruction	Entertainment	Description

	1
16 marks	

2 After each text, explain its main purpose using examples from the text in your answer.

a) Elephants are similar in many ways to humans. They have a similar life span (over 70 years) and reach puberty at roughly the same age – around 13 years old. In addition, females can give birth until they are about 50 years old. They usually produce one calf at a time, but may have twins. Also, elephants live in family groups.

_____

_____

_____

_____

	2a
2 marks	

b) This child needs you! Mia lives in a hovel in central Africa. Her village has no water supply and she has to carry water from a waterhole three miles away. There is no sanitation in the village and many children die for the lack of simple basic hygiene. With a little education, we could save the lives of children such as Mia. For only 50p a day you could make a lasting difference to Mia and other children just like her. Complete and return this slip to the address below today, and we will do the rest for you.

_____

_____

_____

_____

	2b
2 marks	

c) A dirty chain makes riding your bike harder work. There are a few simple steps to cleaning the chain:

      1. Soak a sponge in warm soapy water.
      2. Wrap the sponge around your chain and backpedal a few times.
      3. Repeat until the sponge stays clean.
      4. Dry with a clean rag and then sparingly oil the pins on your chain.

_____

_____

_____

_____

	2c
2 marks	

	/22
Total for this test	

> ## At Level 6 pupils should know that:
> - The author's viewpoint shows the writer's opinion and what he or she thinks about the topic.
> - The beliefs and sympathies of the writer can lead to hidden messages in the text.

Clues about the writer

These can be gathered from various elements of the writing, including:

- the content of the writing
- the words chosen to express emotions
- opinions stated or withheld
- the target audience
- the characters treated sympathetically
- the grammatical structures and vocabulary.

Sometimes information can be explicit and at other times it is necessary to use inference skills to gather support ideas. For example:

> *It was a glorious spectacle. The finest men in the country gathered on the moor, prepared to take the steps necessary to defend their honour and protect their families. As the King rode into their midst, a mighty roar of approval ascended to the heavens. It was a great day for England.*

We can deduce that there is going to be a battle. The writer's approval is signalled in words such as 'glorious', 'finest', 'necessary', 'defend', 'protect', 'approval', 'heavens', 'great day'.

In the classroom

Activity 1

> Give pupils a copy of a sports report from a newspaper. Ask them to read it and highlight words and phrases that indicate the writer's view of the event and those of the participants.

> Compare and discuss responses.

> From this, ask pupils to create a list of information about the writer.

> This exercise can be repeated with different articles.

Activity 2

> Give pupils the roles of different characters in a situation (e.g. children kick a ball through a neighbour's window – pupils can imagine they are the neighbours, a parent, one of the children, a policeman, a witness) and ask them to discuss in pairs and then write about the situation from the viewpoint of that person.

> Pupils read their accounts and then other pupils make notes about what their character is like, based on the evidence read out.

Sample answers (answers will vary)

1. a) disastrous b) enterprising c) well-deserved d) lucky

2. 1 mark for each correct line.

What the text says	What that tells us about the writer
Cycling is a fantastic sport	approves of cycling
foolish cyclists … riding … without helmets	thinks it is silly not to wear a helmet
busy main roads … inviting disaster … risk	considers roads to be dangerous for cyclists
legal requirement	thinks the government should act

3. 1 mark for viewpoint, up to 2 marks for carefully reasoned argument supported by text.
   Disapproves – 'irony', 'greatest injustices', 'freedom-loving animals', 'forced', 'small', 'enforced imprisonment'; thinks people should act – 'people who should know better', 'very right-thinking person'.

1 Circle the word that reflects the author's viewpoint in the following statements.

a) The government is discussing a disastrous policy to test children every six weeks.

b) The government is discussing an enterprising policy to test children every six weeks.

c) Buxworth Blues had a well-deserved win against Whaley Whites.

d) Buxworth Blues had a lucky win against Whaley Whites.

1
4 marks

2 Read the text and complete the table.

Cycling is a fantastic sport that is becoming more popular. However, there are some foolish cyclists who do not consider either their own safety or that of other road users. By riding along busy main roads without helmets they are inviting disaster. Even on quiet country roads, there is a risk that a vehicle could appear, so cyclists should always wear the correct protective gear. It really is time that wearing helmets became a legal requirement.

What the text says	What that tells us about the writer

2
4 marks

3 Read the text and then explain how the writer feels about zoos. Use the text to support your answer.

Linter Zoo is situated in a beautiful part of the city, near the historic court hall. What irony that, in the shadow of a place where justice is celebrated, one of the greatest injustices of our time is smiled upon by the city's inhabitants. Freedom-loving animals are forced to live in small enclosures for the entertainment of people who should know better. Wild animals belong in their natural habitat, where they can roam freely, hunt for their chosen foods, live in their preferred groups and rear their young as nature intended. Every right-thinking person should take a stand against their enforced imprisonment.

3
3 marks

_____

_____

_____

_____

_____

_____

/11

Total for this test

> ## At Level 6 pupils should know that:
> * Personality is the most important aspect of a character description.

Gathering information about a character

Explicit information – information that the writer gives the reader directly:

> *Gill was the cleverest girl in the class, and modest too.*

Implicit information – this information is inferred, leaving more to the imagination and the skill of the reader to understand the character:

> *Gill was always surprised she got top marks in tests at school.*

The main strands of evidence about characters are:
* what they do
* what they say
* what others say about them.

These are further strands to consider.
* what they think
* how others react to them
* how they feel
* how they react to others
* how they move.

Questions related to character

These questions focus on what the character is like, how the writer conveys this to the reader, reasons for character actions and reactions, expectations of character behaviour, how and why the character changes over the course of the story and how the writer varies the style for different character viewpoints.

Answering questions about character

Answers should focus on one facet of character at a time. Assertions about character must be supported by evidence from the text, which will then have to be explained to show that it is understood.

In the classroom

> List some possible character traits on the whiteboard.

> Ask pupils as pairs to select a trait without revealing it to anyone else.

> Pupils prepare and then present to the class examples of what a character might do or say to reveal the chosen character trait, without using the word or other words related to it. For example:
> > *Mean: 'I think your party was rubbish.'*
> > *Scribbling on work and laughing.*

> Discuss examples which worked well.

Sample answers (answers will vary)

1. **a)** Pay for the broken window. 'I'm really sorry.' **b)** fear **c)** excitement **d)** Walked home alone. 'I want a friend.' **e)** greed **f)** anger **g)** curious
2. 1 mark each, up to 3. determined – carrying on even though tired (wearily, aching, craving sleep); self-driven (task she had set herself); desperate (pushing to the limits, counting how many left); reflective (small voice saying, 'Never again.')
3. **a)** 1 mark for each point which is supported by evidence from the text, up to 3.
   spiteful ('served Lucy right'); uncaring (not bothered that Lucy is crying and alone); devious (he knows Lucy hasn't done it); malicious (smirking and gleeful); ruthless (couldn't let Lucy know)
   b) 1 mark for each point which is supported by evidence from the text, up to 3.
    not a fighter (sitting and crying); no close friends (alone when she is in trouble); intelligent (quickly realises it is Amir); honest (can't understand why the others won't believe her)
   c) Amir had taken the watch.
   d) 1 mark for each point which is supported by evidence from the text, up to 3.
   make things worse for Lucy – plant the watch on her and then punish her because he can't have it now
   (he enjoys seeing others in trouble; he doesn't like Lucy – it serves her right; he's spiteful – glee when the others falsely accuse and punish her)

1 Complete the table.

Character feeling	Character action	Character speech
a) remorse		
b)	Hid in the cupboard.	'I want my mum.'
c)	Bounced around the room.	'We're going on holiday.'
d) loneliness		
e)	Ate sweets straight after a big meal.	'May I have some nuts?'
f)	Pushed someone so hard he fell over.	'Just leave me alone.'
g)	Looked into the secret box.	'Where are you going?'

	1
9 marks	

2

> Wearily, Louise continued the task she had set herself. Aching in mind and body she forced herself to focus. Only four left. Four, and she could allow her body the sleep it craved. Even as she pushed to her limits, a small voice in the corner of her mind was whispering, 'Never again.'

What does the extract reveal about Louise's personality?

_____

_____

_____

	2
3 marks	

3

> Amir smirked. It served Lucy right if the others wouldn't talk to her. Lucy sat in the corner with tears pouring down her face. She hadn't taken the watch, so who had? And why would nobody believe her? Then she looked towards Amir. He wasn't quick enough to turn away before she saw the glee in his eye, and then Lucy knew. Well, Amir couldn't have that!

a) What does the text reveal about Amir's character?

_____

_____

	3a
3 marks	

b) What does the text reveal about Lucy's character?

_____

_____

	3b
3 marks	

c) Towards the end of the extract, what do you think it was that Lucy 'knew'?

_____

	3c
1 mark	

d) What do you think Amir will do now? Support your answer with evidence from the text.

_____

_____

_____

	3d
3 marks	

	/22
Total for this test	

At Level 6 pupils should know that:

• A good writer makes structural choices that support the theme and purpose of the text.

Aspects of text organisation

When considering text organisation, it is helpful to consider:
- the paragraph / section order
- connectives (links in and between paragraphs creating textual cohesion)
- how key points are developed
- the presentation method.

Main types of presentation method

Description (e.g. the geography of France)

Cause and effect (e.g. why there was a tsunami in Thailand)

Comparison (e.g. the musical careers of Mozart and Beethoven)

Balanced argument / argument and counter-argument (e.g. the points for and against wearing school uniform)

Sequence (chronological or order) (e.g. events leading up to World War I)

Problem solving (e.g. pollution from cars, possible solutions and effects of the solutions)

Point and evidence (e.g. why animals should be left in the wild)

Question and answer (e.g. a form of point and evidence that can be used for most topics)

Narrative (e.g. setting, problem, action and resolution)

In the classroom

Activity 1

Ask pupils what is meant by text organisation (they should relate this to the planning they do for writing).

Explain that text organisation is used to suit the purpose of the writing. Compare it to types of transport and how they are chosen to suit their purpose – a bus to move more people, a lorry to carry large loads, a sports car to be stylish (or flashy!), a boat to sail on water and so on.

Build up a list of the types of organisation with which pupils are familiar (instructions, story writing, descriptions …). Then look through non-fiction books to find other types of textual organisation that can be added to the list (you may wish to prepare texts beforehand to ensure you have all the examples needed).

In each case, discuss why the writer used that type of organisation and how and why it suited his or her purpose, theme and audience. Results can be recorded in a table.

Activity 2

Ask pupils to devise diagrams to illustrate each type of textual organisation.

Sample answers (answers will vary)

1. a) sequence b) balanced argument c) point and evidence d) cause and effect
2. 1 mark for organisation, up to 2 marks for reasons supporting opinion.
   a) description; yes; it gives a picture of the school situation and the problems that there were (old buildings, structural dangers and faults)
   b) cause and effect (or point and evidence); yes; it shows why safety was a concern and highlights areas where pupils could be at risk (toilets, between buildings)
   c) chronological sequence; yes; it shows the timescale of the new build (1993–2002)
   d) question and answer; no; it doesn't really suit the material in the text, the questions do not make the material easier to understand

24

1 Join each diagram to the organisational method it best illustrates.

a)

1904 1937 1953

b)

description
cause and effect
comparison
balanced argument
sequence
problem solving
point and evidence
question and answer
narrative

c)

d)

	1
4 marks	

2 For each paragraph, state the organisational method, evaluate the suitability and give reasons to support your answer.

a) The vision for a new school in Buxworth was born over 30 years ago. At the time, the school consisted of the original school building, which housed the hall and a room used for pre-school; a 1930s Nissan hut, which was held up inside by scaffolding poles and housed two classes; and a 1950s temporary classroom which leaked in winter and roasted children in the summer. The toilets were in a separate building at the edge of the small playground.

Text organisation _____ Suitability _____

Reason(s) _____

_____

2a
3 marks

b) A visit from Ofsted highlighted some safety issues. The entrance to the boys' toilet could not be seen from any classroom and there was only a limited view of the girls' entrance. This meant pupils going to the toilets in lesson time could be at risk. The school site could not be secured because there was a public footpath cutting through part of it and buildings needed to be open to allow pupil access. This all resulted in pupil safety being a concern.

Text organisation _____ Suitability _____

Reason(s) _____

_____

2b
3 marks

c) In 1993, when money was allocated for updating school buildings, the first bid for a new build was put to the government. It was rejected and resubmitted in 1994. This time it was passed but there were insufficient funds to go ahead. However, in 1999 plans were finally made to replace the building. Work started in 2000 and was completed in 2002.

Text organisation _____ Suitability _____

Reason(s) _____

_____

2c
3 marks

d) Was the new school necessary? Yes, the old school was unsuitable and unsafe. Why did a small school justify this expenditure? Because a school is at the heart of the local community. Do the children appreciate their new facilities? They absolutely love everything about the school – after all, they *are* the school.

Text organisation _____ Suitability _____

Reason(s) _____

_____

2d
3 marks

/16

Total for this test

> **At Level 6 pupils should know that:**
> - Features at text level include layout headings, language, text style, illustrations, design and the type of information.
> - The type of text can dictate the features that are used

Features that can be used

Layout – relates to how the text is set out on the page.

Language – the vocabulary and sentence structures are often dictated by the target audience.

Text style – includes eye-catching fonts (typefaces), different text sizes, bold, italics and underlining.

Illustrations – can be photographs, pictures or diagrams.

Why these features are used

These features are used to make the text attractive and accessible to the reader. The way in which the features are used usually indicates the target audience. For example, short sections of text in simple language with lots of illustrations would be used for a child's reference book. The features used can sometimes be indicative of the type of text (for example, instructions or poetry).

Questions related to text features

These questions usually relate to how the features contribute to the effects achieved within the text.

Answering questions related to text features

It is not sufficient to answer these questions with a general answer such as 'for impact' or 'because they are instructions'. The answers require an explanation of the part each feature plays in communicating with the reader. Consider:

How does the layout of this page engage the reader?

Answer: The heading is larger and states the purpose of the text. Key points are highlighted and there are clear subheadings so readers can select the sections they are interested in. Teaching steps are suggested and numbered.

In the classroom

> Have a variety of texts available. Give pupils some time to examine the different texts.

> Ask pupils to list the features they can find in each text.

> Examine each text in turn and work through the list of features, giving pupils the opportunity to explain why the feature is used in that text (answers will relate to the intended audience and the purpose of the text).

Sample answers (answers will vary)

1. 1 mark for two features, 3 marks for more than three per box.
   a) start text with a list of equipment, method written in numbered points, imperative verbs used
   b) address of sender in the top right, date beneath, address where sent next on the left, main letter starts with Dear …, the text is then in paragraphs using formal language, signed off formally at the end
   c) text in blocks, illustrations and diagrams, headings and subheadings larger text, lists
   d) paragraphs, figurative language, complex sentence structures
   e) larger text, not much text on a page, bright illustrations, simple language and sentence structures
   f) clear title, text set in short lines and maybe verses, figurative language, phrases and clauses not necessarily as complete sentences.

2. bold, italics, boxed text

3. 1 mark for each feature with a reason, up to 4.
   Larger, bold, eye-catching title more specific to content, subheadings for paragraphs, diagrams to clarify the meaning, numbered demonstration of finding an interval.

1 In the boxes, list the features you would expect in each of the texts.

a) Instructions	b) Letter of complaint
c) Information page	d) Description
e) Story for young children	f) Poem

18 marks   1

2 Give three features that might be used to emphasise important points in a text.

a) _____

b) _____

c) _____

3 marks   2

3 How could the features of this text be improved for pupils in your class?

> **Music**
> Music is written on a set of five lines called a stave. Notes can be written on any of the lines or above or below the lines. The distance between two notes is called an interval. To work out the interval between two notes, count the lower note as one and then count each line and space up to the other note. If you counted to five, the interval would be a fifth.
>
> Chords are made by putting notes together. The most common chord uses the intervals of a first and a third and a fifth. This is called a root position chord. In a chord the notes are all played at the same time.

_____

_____

_____

_____

_____

_____

_____

_____

_____

4 marks   3

/25

Total for this test

> ## At Level 6 pupils should know that:
> - The style of writing is how an author writes to the audience.
> - Style can reveal a writer's personality and viewpoints.

Influences on stylistic choices

Some of the factors that influence the style of a piece of writing are:
- the purpose of the text (think about the styles used for a letter of complaint, a letter to support a job application and a letter of condolence)
- the situation of the writer (constraints placed by the text and personal circumstances)
- cultural influences (the periodic sentence – a long sentence that has the main point at the end –was popular in classical times!)
- the need to avoid monotony.

Stylist features

Some of the features that indicate the style of writing are:
- sentence structure (simple, complex and compound sentences)
- language choices (technical, colloquial, figurative, emotive)
    - ➤ connotation – words that can have different associations for different people (e.g. home). The writer can guide the reader's interpretation to some extent and choose words deliberately to suit his or her purpose.
    - ➤ clichés – overused sayings (e.g. all dressed up and nowhere to go) that some people prefer not to use
- level of formality
- bias, balance or neutral stance.

In the classroom

Activity 1 – examining texts

Have a variety of texts available. Give pupils some time to examine the different texts.

⬇

Ask pupils to describe the style of each text.

⬇

Examine each text in turn and work through the list of stylistic features, giving pupils the opportunity to explain why the feature is used in that text (answers will relate to the intended audience and the purpose of the text).

Activity 2 – examining parts of texts

Take two separate sentences from each of a variety of texts. Give pupils the sentence pairs and ask them to match the sentences that would come from the same text (beware of font differences!) and then decide what type of text it would be.

⬇

Discuss responses.

Sample answers (answers will vary)

1.

Text type	Sentence structure	Language choices	Level of formality	Level of bias
Formal letter of complaint	mainly complex and compound	technical, no contractions, imperative, forceful, emotive	very formal	towards own viewpoint, but trying to appear objective
Children's story book	mainly simple	simple, emotive	fairly informal	towards the main character
Instructions	simple	imperative verbs, technical	very	neutral
Business report in a newspaper	complex and compound	technical and not emotive	very	balanced
Report about a local festival in a newspaper	mixed	friendly, emotive, figurative	fairly informal	strong positive viewpoint
Humorous novel	mixed	puns, figurative, idioms,	fairly informal	towards the main character
Scientific report	complex and compound	technical, not emotive	very	balanced

2.

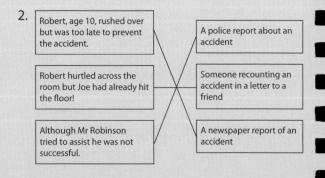

3. i and iv ticked

1 Complete the table to show the stylistic features you would expect to find in these texts.

Text type	Sentence structure	Language choices	Level of formality	Level of bias
Formal letter of complaint				
Children's story book				
Instructions				
Business report in a newspaper				
Report about a local festival in a newspaper				
Humorous novel				
Scientific report				

1
28 marks

2 Match these sentences to the text from which they are most likely to have been taken.

Robert, age 10, rushed over but was too late to prevent the accident.	A police report about an accident
Robert hurtled across the room but Joe had already hit the floor!	Someone recounting an accident in a letter to a friend
Although Mr Robinson tried to assist he was not successful.	A newspaper report of an accident

2
3 marks

3 Tick the two of the following sentences that might be from an instruction manual for a new alarm system.

    i) Pressing the yellow button activates the automated voice recorder.

    ii) Pressing the green button resulted in a terrifying wailing sound.

    iii) Deactivate the system with your gun.

    iv) Engage the warning system by setting the timer to 10 seconds.

3
2 marks

/33
Total for this test

At Level 6 pupils should know that:
- Choice of sentence structure is influenced by the style, purpose and intended audience.
- Sentence structure affects the rhythm and pace of the writing.

Possible sentence structures

Type	Structure	Use	Example
Simple	1 independent clause, although it can have a compound subject and verb	• to convey urgency, shock, fear or surprise • for imperative instruction • to emphasise an idea • for clarity, simplicity and normality • to increase the pace	*Jack ran down the hill.*
Compound	2+ independent clauses joined with a semi-colon or a co-ordinating conjunction	• to draw together two equal ideas • to link ideas • to add extra information • to help writing flow	*Andy went out running and I read a book.* (Coordinating conjuctions are: for, and, nor, but, or, yet, so. Remember them with the mnemonic **FANBOYS**.)
Complex	1 independent clause and 1+ dependent clause joined by a subordinating conjunction	• to add extra layers of meaning • to add extra information • to add variety and contrast • for more complex ideas • for more sophisticated descriptions • to develop ideas	*Whenever it is sunny, I like to spend some time in the garden although I don't really have time.*
Compound-complex	2+ independent clauses and 1+ dependent clause	• as complex sentences	*My car failed its MOT because it needed new tyres and they cost £400!*

In the classroom

Check that pupils are familiar with simple, compound and complex sentences.

Show pupils a page of text and ask them to tally the sentence types in the text (they will count compound-complex as complex, which is acceptable at this stage).

Discuss why the text has the proportion of each type of sentence (this will reflect the purpose and intended audience).

Examine each sentence individually and discuss what purpose that sentence serves in the text and why it was selected by the writer.

Sample answers (answers will vary)

1. a) C b) X c) S d) C e) S f) X
2. simple sentence: a, d, h, (g), j, m, o; compound sentence: b, f, (g), l, n; complex sentence: c, e, g, (i), k, l
3. a – iv; b – iii; c – i; d – ii; e – vii; f – vi; g – v
   When I am older I would like to be an architect. I love looking at buildings and thinking about how to improve them. Architecture is fascinating.

1 Write an **S** by each simple sentence, a **C** by each compound sentence and an **X** by each complex sentence.

a) He wouldn't let us go out, yet he went off up the hill.

b) I like to go to the theatre whenever the play is a comedy.

c) The man jumped.

d) Peter wanted to see what the problem was but Max wouldn't let him.

e) We talked and laughed all the way there.

f) We went for a meal after we had been on the ski slope.

1

6 marks

2 Match the purposes of the sentence to the most suitable sentence type.

a) to increase the pace

b) to show two ideas are   equal

c) for extra layers of meaning

d) an imperative instruction

e) for more complex ideas

f) to improve the flow

g) to add variety

h) for clarity

simple sentence

compound sentence

complex sentence

i) to add extra information

j) to shock

k) for more sophisticated descriptions

l) to develop more complicated thoughts

m) for simplicity

n) to link ideas

o) to show fear

2

15 marks

3 Match the sentence halves to learn about how and why to use different sentence types.

a) A variety of sentence types

b) All your writing should

c) Long complicated sentences

d) Your choice of sentence type

e) Lots of simple sentences

f) Simple, short sentences after longer sentences

g) Every sentence should

i) are more difficult to understand.

ii) depends on your audience and the purpose of the text.

iii) have a mixture of sentence types.

iv) makes text more interesting.

v) give the reader a message.

vi) have a big impact.

vii) sound too choppy.

3

7 marks

4 Write three sentences about your ambitions using a simple, compound and complex sentence.

_____

_____

_____

4

3 marks

/31

Total for this test

At Level 6 pupils should know that:

- Figurative language includes the use of similes, metaphors, personification, alliteration, onomatopoeia, hyperbole and idioms.
- In reading, it is important to focus on the reason for the figurative language.

Definitions of figurative language

Simile: comparing one thing to another (as black as soot)
Metaphor: saying one thing is another (the car was a beast)
Personification: giving an object human characteristics (the sun smiled)
Alliteration: using repeated letter sounds to create effect (slow snaking slalom)
Onomatopoeia: using words that sound like what they name (Crash!)
Hyperbole: using gross exaggeration (I could eat a horse)
Idiom: using words and sayings beyond their literal meaning (being under the weather)

Why writers use figurative language

Writers use figurative language to help their readers understand the image they are trying to create. By using imagery and sensory words, the writer allows the reader to draw on previous knowledge and experience to gain a deeper understanding of the text.

Questions related to figurative language

These questions tend to ask why certain phrases were used or why they were effective. Questions may be less directed, such as asking how the author made the description effective.

Answering questions related to figurative language

It is not sufficient to answer these questions with general answers such as 'for impact' or 'to help the reader know what it was like', or even 'because it was a metaphor'. Whilst it is good to show you know the type of language used, the answer requires an explanation of what the writer was trying to convey to the reader. Consider:

Why does the author say: *Wind crept out along the forest floor.*

Answer: To show that the wind was low to the ground but not very strong. By personifying the wind in this way he made it seem like a weak, fearful thing.

In the classroom

Show pupils examples of figurative language (either as isolated sentences or within descriptive texts).

⬇

Look at the first sentence together. Discuss why the writer used that language and what picture was being created. How effective is the example and why?

⬇

Ask pupils to work in pairs and discuss the other sentences, deciding why the writer uses that particular type of language.

⬇

Compare responses and discuss.

⬇

Consider which examples work particularly well and which ones don't.

Sample answers (answers will vary)

1. 1 mark for type of figurative language, 2 marks for reason for use.
   a) metaphor; to show he rushed and caused chaos, knocking things over and startling people **b)** alliteration; the repeated use of *p* mimics the sound and rhythm of the woodpecker pecking **c)** simile; to show that the wolf was timid and wary, cowering away from people **d)** hyperbole; to show that the cake really was big **e)** onomatopoeia; the words about how the man spoke are like the sounds he made **f)** personification; to show that the sound of the music was tempting the writer to dance, like someone trying to persuade
2. 1 mark for each point which is supported by evidence from the text, up to 4.
   'like a frosty morning', shows it was cold, crisp and clear, with the cold making your cheeks go red. 'whizz' and 'race track' show that the skaters are moving really quickly but there are 'unwary children' playing who keep getting in the way – 'stumbled onto the track'. The writer expects to be able to skate 'confidently' but can't – 'like a new-born foal' that can't stand properly and 'bewilderment' shows surprise at falling over.

1 Read these sentences. Name and underline the type of figurative language used and explain why it was used.

a) The man was a hurricane, dashing through the office to the door.

Figurative language: _____

Reason for use: _____

_____

b) The woodpecker pecked people persistently purposely pestering them.

Figurative language: _____

Reason for use: _____

_____

c) The wolf was like a frightened rabbit.

Figurative language: _____

Reason for use: _____

_____

d) The cake was as big as our classroom!

Figurative language: _____

Reason for use: _____

_____

e) The man hissed and whispered to us.

Figurative language: _____

Reason for use: _____

_____

f) The music whispered enticingly, inviting me to dance.

Figurative language: _____

Reason for use: _____

_____

	1
	18 marks

2 Read this text.

> Ice cold entered my nose like a frosty morning, only with a sour taste. Cold air brushed my cheeks, leaving them tingling and flushed. I watched skaters whizz by, a flurry of smiles and shouts as unwary children stumbled onto the race track. I stepped onto the ice and pushed off confidently. Then I was like a new-born foal, trying to find and control my legs as they disappeared in different directions, leaving me a soft heap of bewilderment on the ice.

Explain how the writer helps the reader to understand what it was like at the skating rink.

_____

_____

_____

_____

_____

_____

	2
	4 marks

/22
Total for this test

> **At Level 6 pupils should know that:**
> - Techniques to influence the reader include the personal pronouns, rhetorical questions, repetition, emotive language and provoking empathy.
> - These are all persuasive devices.

Definitions of techniques to influence the reader

Pronouns: the use of pronouns, such as you, we, us, our, to involve the reader.

Rhetorical questions: questions that don't need an answer and so imply that the writer is correct.

Repetition: reinforces and emphasises the main message.

Emotive language: words like horrific, heroic, historic, terrified, mob, refused).

Provoking empathy: helps the reader to understand and share feelings.

Questions related to techniques to influence the reader

These tend to ask why certain phrases were used or were effective. Questions may be less directed, such as asking how the reader is persuaded to take the writer's viewpoint.

Answering questions about techniques to influence the reader

It is not sufficient to answer these questions with general statements such as 'to persuade the reader', or 'because it was a rhetorical question'. Whilst it is good to show the type of language used is known, the answer requires an explanation of how the writer is influencing the reader. Consider:

Why does the author say: *Do you think it is right that children are brutally exploited in these labour camps?*

Answer: He is using pronouns such as 'you' to make the matter personal to the reader; there are emotive words like 'brutally exploited' that make it difficult to disagree with the wider argument; the reader is being asked a rhetorical question – no one would answer yes to this, so the reader has to agree with the writer.

In the classroom

> Show pupils examples of language intended to influence the reader (either as isolated sentences or within texts).

> Look at the first sentence together. Discuss why the writer uses that language and how the writer is attempting to influence the reader. Is the example effective and why?

> Ask pupils to work in pairs and discuss the other sentences, deciding why the writer uses each particular technique.

> Compare responses and discuss.

> Consider which examples work particularly well and which ones don't.

Sample answers (answers will vary)

1. 1 mark for language feature, 2 marks for reason for use.
   a) emotive language, rhetorical question, personal pronoun; use of negative emotive words such as 'disgusting' and 'soiled' means that the reader will answer no to the personal question b) emotive language, personal pronouns; 'rioters' and 'threatening' make the reader feel unsafe and this is compounded by the mention of families c) empathy; everyone knows what it is like to feel lonely so this makes the reader sympathetic to Cydney even if she is being bad d) repetition, emotive words; the words are all negative and strong and the effect builds through the sentences, so that the reader agrees with the last statement e) emotive words, personally pronouns; 'considerate' and 'dedicated' are qualities to be valued and this is reinforced by the word 'deserves' so readers are inclined to think positively about the woman

2. 1 mark for each point which is supported by evidence from the text, up to 4.
   The writer draws the reader in with two personal questions to which everyone will give the same answer. She then uses emotive language, including 'impoverished', 'condemning', 'deprivation', 'hardship' and 'poverty' to gain the reader's sympathy and then inserts a rhetorical question that pushes the reader to take her view, followed by an appeal for money, making it difficult for the reader to refuse. Saying 'don't turn your back' implies that only heartless people wouldn't respond.

1 Read these sentences. Underline and name all the language features that are used to influence the reader and explain why they were used.

a) Cramped, soiled and disgusting – would you keep a dog in those conditions?

Language features: _____

Reason for use: _____

_____

1a
3 marks

b) The rioters are threatening the safety of our families.

Language features: _____

Reason for use: _____

_____

1b
3 marks

c) Cydney only started to misbehave when she was lonely because her best friend left.

Language features: _____

Reason for use: _____

_____

1c
3 marks

d) It's wrong. It's unfair. It's biased. It's unjust. It's disgraceful!

Language features: _____

Reason for use: _____

_____

1d
3 marks

e) Such a considerate, dedicated woman deserves our vote today.

Language features: _____

Reason for use: _____

_____

1e
3 marks

2 Read this text.

> Do you ever complain about attending school? But you want to get a good job as an adult, right? Well, there are millions of children who do not get the opportunity to attend school. Lots of countries (especially poor ones) charge for children to go to school, which means impoverished families cannot afford to send their children. Consequently, more than ten percent of children in these countries are illiterate, condemning them to a life of continued hardship, deprivation and poverty. Wouldn't it be great if we could help those children? Well you can! For just £10 a month you can guarantee a new life by paying the school fees for one of these children. Don't turn your back – don't waste a moment – send the money now.

How is the writer influencing the reader?

_____

_____

_____

_____

_____

_____

2
4 marks

/19

Total for this test

Definitions of techniques to convey humour

Alliteration: using repeated letter sounds to create effect (*slow snaking slalom*).

Irony: saying the opposite of what is meant (*Great!*).

Hyperbole: using gross exaggeration (*I could eat a horse*).

Understatement: saying less than is meant (Titanic – *We're taking in a little water*).

Rhetorical questions: questions where an answer is not expected (*Is the Pope Catholic?*).

Self-deprecation: belittling or under-valuing oneself (concert pianist – *I play a little*).

Humorous writing

When looking for the humour in writing, look for the normal, balanced ordinary person or situation and then the contrasting absurd or fantastical person or situation. It is usually the conflict between these two that creates much of the humour.

Questions related to humorous language

These questions ask why certain phrases are humorous or why they are effective. Questions may be less directed, such as asking how the author made the text humorous.

Answering questions related to humorous language

It is not sufficient to answer these questions with general answers such as 'it's funny' or 'to make the reader laugh', or even 'because it is hyperbole'. The answer requires an explanation of what the writer was trying to convey to the reader. Consider:

Why does the author say: *'Camping! Oh great. I can't wait,' said Gill.*

Answer: To show that Gill did not want to go camping because when she says 'Oh great' you know she is being sarcastic and 'I can't wait' is irony because she means she would prefer to wait forever and not go.

In the classroom

Show pupils examples of humorous language (either as isolated sentences or within texts).

⬇

Look at the first sentence together. Discuss why the writer used that language and how humour is being created and used. How effective is the example and why?

⬇

Ask pupils to work in pairs and discuss the other sentences, deciding why the writer uses that particular type of language.

⬇

Compare responses and discuss.

⬇

Consider which examples work particularly well and which ones don't.

(1) Explain the humour in each of these pictures.

a)
_____

_____

b)
_____

_____

	1
	4 marks

c)
_____

_____

d)
_____

_____

(2) Read these sentences. Underline and name the humorous language used and explain why it was used.

a) Did I want to go to the concert? I mean, is the grass green?

Humorous language: _____

Reason for use: _____

_____

	2a
	3 marks

b) 'We seem to have a little leak,' said Jake, as the water cascaded down the stairs.

Humorous language: _____

Reason for use: _____

_____

	2b
	3 marks

c) When he was asked if the surgeon could clean his grazed knee, the surgeon replied, 'I think I might manage.'

Humorous language: _____

Reason for use: _____

_____

	2c
	3 marks

d) 'You exaggerate a million times a day,' said his sister.

Humorous language: _____

Reason for use: _____

	2d
	3 marks

	2e
	3 marks

e) Mr Sellers put a notice on his classroom wall: | CORRECT SPELLLING IS IMPORTANT |

Humorous language: _____

Reason for use: _____

	/19

Total for this test

> ## At Level 6 pupils should know that:
> - Readers' responses to a text are a reflection of their opinion of what they have read.
> - Writers are trying to elicit a response from their readers.

Responses to texts

Different people react differently to different texts. Because of personality and past experience some readers will respond in ways that the writer was not expecting or intending.

Features that writers use to elicit a response

Features that can be used to elicit a response include:

- powerful verbs
- creating atmospheres
- vivid descriptions
- changes in pace
- strong personalities
- emotive language
- using punctuation to draw reader attention!
- rhetorical questions
- direct address to the reader.

Questions related to the reader's response

These questions often ask directly for an opinion on information contained within the text and how the writer has achieved that response. Questions can also relate to what response the writer is trying to elicit.

Answering questions related to the reader's response

Even if pupils don't have any particular response, they are asked to identify what response the writer was intending to create and that should be the focus of any answer, rather than their own lack of response.

In the classroom

Give pupils some short sections of descriptive text (which could include poetry).

Ask them to read each text and then discuss with their partner how the writer is trying to make the reader feel and note the response on the appropriate text.

Collect response words and display them on the whiteboard (angry, jealous, anxious, curious, fearful, excited ...).

Ask pupils to discuss with their partner how the writer has elicited that response. They could underline the key words and features on each text.

Collect responses and discuss.

Frame questions for pupils that can be answered using the annotations on each text. (*How does the writer make the reader feel fearful? How does the writer's choice of vocabulary help the reader feel excited?*) The questions can be answered orally and may be discussed with a partner first.

Sample answers (answers will vary)

1. suspense – short simple sentences that emphasise the waiting and language choices of 'still' and 'tense'; curious – what is the shadow and why are they waiting?
2. 1 mark for each point which is supported by evidence from the text, up to 2.

   slow, warm, carefree day with the sigh of tranquillity all around it; uses alliteration and rhyme to create a gentle, swinging rhythm; word choices – 'warmth', 'comfort'
3. 1 mark for each point which is supported by evidence from the text, up to 2.
   a) rhetorical questions, implication that Joe knows it was a silly thing to do and a reminder that we've all done silly things
   b) curiosity – was he badly hurt? Was the car driver hurt? What did the others do? Did the car stop? Did they know 'that car'? Did they know the driver?
4. a) 1 mark for each point which is supported by evidence from the text, up to 3.
      strong emotive words ('criminal', 'exploited', 'deprived', 'starved', 'imprisoned', 'fearfully', 'toil') make the reader feel sorry for the children; knowing such treatment is wrong – 'outrage'
   b) Full explanation 2 marks, award 1 mark for a fair attempt.
      to persuade the reader that buying cheap goods from this source is wrong
5. 1 mark for each point which is supported by evidence from the text, up to 3.
   'ride was a monster'; creates excitement tinged with fear because monsters are fearful but a ride is fun, so the ride must be frightening. The verbs 'rearing', 'bucking', 'tossing' and 'grabbing' convey the movements of the ride. This makes it sound exciting – and the riders are 'exhilarated' afterwards.

1

> We waited, still and tense. The shadow moved. And moved again.

The writer makes the reader feel _____ by _____

_____

	1

2 marks

2

> Tranquillity. In a lush, lazy, hazy world of colour I relaxed into the warmth and comfort of the sun without a care. Tranquillity.

What atmosphere does the writer's use of language create? Refer to the text in your answer.

_____

_____

	2

2 marks

3

> We've all done silly things at some time, haven't we? Things that we want to forget as soon as possible? Well, that's how Joe felt after the accident. All the kids had been trying it – seeing how far down the road we could ride without touching our handle bars. Tom had reached the bridge, and that's what prompted Joe to push himself further than before. He was going really well until that car appeared around the corner …

a) How does the writer make the reader feel empathy with Joe?

_____

_____

	3a

2 marks

b) What response does the reader have to the unfinished sentence at the end of the text?

_____

_____

	3b

2 marks

4

> It is criminal that children so young are exploited to produce cheap clothes and toys for people who live in a rich country like ours. Deprived, starving and virtually imprisoned, children fearfully force themselves to toil through the day, continually anticipating a blow from an unsatisfied supervisor.

a) Comment on the emotive language used and the effect that it has on the reader.

_____

_____

	4a

3 marks

b) In your opinion, why has the writer used these words?

_____

_____

	4b

2 marks

5

> The ride was a monster, rearing and bucking, tossing its victims away before grabbing them closer, oblivious to their screams, intent only on catching more prey, as they idled past, casting curious glances towards it. With a final bellow it lowered its head and disgorged a laughing, heaving mob of exhilarated people and, with a satisfied smirk, turned its attention to its next meal.

What metaphor does the writer use and what is the effect on the reader?

_____

_____

_____

_____

	5

3 marks

	/16

Total for this test

> **At Level 6 pupils should know that:**
> - Poetry is a form of written communication that can often be understood on many different levels.

Poetry

Poetry offers an excellent vehicle for stretching and stimulating Level 6 pupils. Within a short piece of text there are opportunities to explore language choices and order, layers of meaning, rhythm and patterning. Studying elements of a poem can be fitted into a few minutes or used for extended work. Pupils can imitate poems and experiment with language in a concise form of expression.

Questions related to poetry

These focus on what the poet is trying to say, how they are communicating that message and the effect this may have on the reader.

Answering questions about text purpose

When writing about what a poet is trying to say, focus on the images and descriptions used, and on the atmosphere the poet is trying to create. Remember to refer to the text. This can involve naming language features *and saying why they are used*, quoting from the text *and explaining the relevance of the quote*, referring to text features such as layout and punctuation *and saying why the poet has used them*. So the response pattern should be:

1. what the poet is trying to communicate
2. use of the text to exemplify this, perhaps naming the feature used as well
3. an explanation of how that achieves the purpose.

In the classroom

> Read a poem with the pupils.

⇩

> Ask pupils to list the images, atmosphere and emphasis of the poem.

⇩

> Collect the responses and discuss.

⇩

> Ask pupils to list features of language (such as metaphors), features of text (such as layout and punctuation), any significant word choices and any use of rhythm and metre.

⇩

> Ask pupils to explain orally how the features identified are used to create the images, atmosphere and emphases in the poem.

⇩

> Discuss responses and stress that responses to poetry are often individual, and that what pupils really need to focus on is what response the writer was trying to elicit (especially if they don't have any particular response to it themselves!).

Sample answers (answers will vary)

1. 1 mark each, up to 2.
   simple four-line verse, simple language, simple message, rhyming couplets, regular rhythm.
2. 1 mark for correct message, 1 mark for quotes from text.
   If you talk about your anger it ends but if you bottle it up (I told it not) it gets worse (did grow). OR We tell friends when they upset us and sort things out but we don't treat others the same so it makes things worse – treat people the same.
3. 1 mark for identify metaphor, 1 mark for each point about effectiveness up to 2.
   the anger is an apple tree; effective because if plants are neglected they die and the same would happen to anger; he looks after it and it grows.
4. 1 mark for each point which is supported by evidence from the text, up to 2.
   His enemy steals the apple because he knows that 'it was mine' (mean) but the poison apple kills him and the narrator was 'glad'.
5. 1 mark for each point which is supported by evidence from the text, up to 3.
   sly – smiles at his foe whilst plotting revenge; malicious – plans for a long time and enjoys it; vengeful / unfeeling – shows no remorse about death; understands people – knows his enemy will steal the fruit
6. 1 mark for each point which is supported by evidence from the text, up to 3.
   EITHER The narrator – not open about what first upset him, feeds anger, pretends to be friends, enjoys planning revenge. OR his enemy – started the feud, comes to steal the fruit. If he hadn't done that, he wouldn't have died

Read the poem and then answer the questions.

A Poison Tree *by William Blake*

I was angry with my friend:
I told my wrath, my wrath did end.
I was angry with my foe:
I told it not, my wrath did grow.

And I watered it in fears,
Night and morning with my tears;
And I sunned it with smiles,
And with soft deceitful wiles.

And it grew both day and night,
Till it bore an apple bright.
And my foe beheld it shine.
And he knew that it was mine,

And into my garden stole
When the night had veiled the pole;
In the morning glad I see
My foe outstretched beneath the tree.

1 Look at the first verse. How does the poet create the feeling of a nursery rhyme?

_____

_____

_____

	1
2 marks

2 Use the text to explain the message that the poet is giving in the first verse.

_____

_____

_____

	2
2 marks

3 Read verses and 3 and 4 (on the right side). What metaphor is the poet using and why is it effective?

_____

_____

_____

	3
3 marks

4 What happened at the end of the poem and how did the narrator feel? Use the text to support your answer.

_____

_____

_____

	4
2 marks

5 What is the character of the narrator and how does the poet show this?

_____

_____

_____

	5
3 marks

6 In your opinion, which character is the to blame for the situation, the narrator or his enemy? Use the text to support your answer.

_____

_____

_____

_____

	6
3 marks

	/15
Total for this test

Features to look for in older texts

Word meanings: these can change over time.

Obsolete words: some words fall out of use or are replaced by new words. The context in which the words are used can sometimes be used to deduce the meaning of words that are unfamiliar.

Spelling variations: spellings were not really fixed until after the advent of the printing press made text more widely available. In older texts spellings are not always consistent even within one text.

Sentence structure: this can change, often to reflect changing speech patterns.

Examples

Look at how the words, spellings and sentence structures have evolved in these lines from different versions of the Lord's Prayer.

A. Fæder ure þu þe eart on heofonum Si þin nama gehalgod (Old English)

B. Oure fadir þat art in heuenes halwid be þi name (Early Middle English)

C. Oure fadir that art in heuenes, halewid be thi name (Later Middle English)

D. Our father which art in heaven, hallowed be thy name (1559)

E. Our father in heaven, may your name be honoured. (modern)

In the classroom

Copy the versions of the Lord's Prayer onto cards, but omit the time indications.

Give pupils card A. Ask them to read it and translate as much as they can into modern English. Repeat with card B, then C and so on. At what stage do pupils recognise the text?

When pupils have all the versions, ask them to underline the word heaven in each version.

Give pupils an unfamiliar text and have them find and point out specified pieces of information as quickly as possible.

Discuss how the word changes and notice its position in the sentence.

Emphasise how the spelling, the word itself and its position in the sentence can all change over time.

Sample answers (answers will vary)

1. a) obsolete words ('trome', 'thurte', 'wicteste'); words spelled differently ('maydnes' = maidens, 'alle' = all, 'litel' = little, 'ani' = any); word order is unusual (a tale that I you will tell)

   b) Listen to me, good men, **wives, maidens and all men, of a story that I will tell** to whoever stays here to listen. **The story is about Havelok; while he was young, he played naked**. Havelok was a really good person, he was really good in every situation; he was the bravest when needed that might ride any horse.

2. a) A–P *Beowulf* (from oral tradition, c 700AD); B–S *Emma* (Jane Austin, written 1815) C–R *Merchant of Venice* (Shakespeare, written between 1596 and 1598); D–Q *Canterbury Tales* (Chaucer, written between 1387 and 1400)

   b) reference to the familiarity of words in the texts with examples (1 mark); reference to the spelling of words with examples (1 mark); reference to un/familiar word order / sentence structure with examples (1 mark).

1 Read the opening of the ballad, *Havelock the Dane*.

Havelok the Dane

Herknet to me, godemen,

Wives, maydnes, and alle men, _____

Of a tale that ich you wile telle, _____

Wo-so it wile here and ther-to duelle.

The tale is of Havelok imaked; _____

Wil he was litel, he yede ful naked. _____

Havelok was a ful god gome:

He was ful god in everi trome;

He was the wicteste man at nede

That thurte riden on ani stede.

a) Give three different features that show the text is old.

i) _____

ii) _____

iii) _____

	1a
3 marks	

b) Work out as much of the modern meaning as you can. Next to each line in bold, write the meaning in modern English.

	1b
4 marks	

2 a) Join these texts to the letters on the timeline to show when they were written.

500 AD	1000 AD	1500 AD	2000 AD
P	Q	R	S

A)	B)	C)	D)
þe hie ær drugon aldorlease lange hwile. Him þæs liffrea, wuldres wealdend, woroldare forgeaf; Beowulf wæs breme (blæd wide sprang), Scyldes eafera Scedelandum in.	If things are going untowardly one month, they are sure to mend the next.	The quality of mercy is not strain'd, It droppeth as the gentle rain from heaven Upon the place beneath. It is twice blest:	His breed, his ale, was alweys after oon, A bettre envyned man was nowher noon. Withoute bake mete was nevere his hous

	2a
4 marks	

b) Give reasons for the order, supporting your answer by referring to the texts.

_____

_____

_____

_____

	2b
3 marks	

	/14
Total for this test	

At Level 6 pupils should know that:

- Different people have different beliefs, customs and ways of life.
- Words can have different meanings in different countries and languages.
- Some parts of the world have names for unfamiliar concepts and objects.

Features of writing from and about other cultures

Usually there are immediate clues that signal that writing is from a different culture. These can include:

- unfamiliar vocabulary
- speech in non-Standard English to reflect the speaker
- different beliefs and rituals are revealed
- different lifestyles and conditions are described
- attitudes to events and situations are different
- descriptions of unusual places.

Within the text, differences and similarities between cultures may be discussed.

In the classroom

Activity 1

Ask pupils to work in pairs and define the terms 'culture' 'beliefs', 'rituals', 'lifestyles', 'living conditions', 'customs' and 'traditional'. Discuss the responses and ensure that all pupils are clear about the meanings of these terms.

Discuss the different cultures that pupils have encountered (at home, school, in their local community, through the media and on holiday).

Establish similarities and differences, ensuring that the differences are respected and accepted.

Make fact sheets displaying information about the different cultures – include all those represented by pupils in the group. Ensure that language and vocabulary form an important part of the sheet.

Activity 2

Present pupils with sentences with similar meanings as they could be said by different people in various parts of the world (all variations and dialects of English). For example, '*The water is in the cooler in the trunk*' (American). '*The water is in the cool-box in the boot*' (English). '*Watar is int' cool-box int' back*' (Yorkshire). '*De wata is in de cooler in de trunk*' (Jamaican).

Discuss similarities and differences.

Use the Internet to search for different dialects (beware of sites that include unsuitable vocabulary) and challenge pupils to create sentences as they might be said in different parts of the English-speaking world.

Sample answers (answers will vary)

1. 2 marks each. a) there are volcanoes; people had been living in tents when their 'home was swept away' for weeks – that wouldn't happen in England because houses are stronger and you would be found somewhere better than a tent to stay; when people speak they use foreign words and phrases.
2. 1 mark for both, 1 mark for supporting evidence from text. a child – she goes to school (because her job has to be before school) and she has to do what her father says – he won't let her learn to play an instrument
3. 3 marks full explanation, 1 mark for evidence from the text, up to 4. The houses are flimsy because it says that one was swept away; lots of the family live together – as well as the parents and children there is at least a grandfather and a pregnant Aunt. The child is expected to help around the house when she isn't at school and working and accepts without question or complaint that she must obey her father.
4. **a)** 1 mark for each term. *Jam karet,* gamelan band, nasi goreng, *Selamet datang, Nyepi* **b)** because most readers would not understand these terms.

Read the following passages and then answer the question.

> I really like our new house. It is closer to the river and further from the volcano. I was glad to leave the tent we have had to use since our home was swept away. This house should have been ready for us weeks ago but father kept saying, '*Jam karet!*' when mother asked about it. It was hard to get grandfather down the hill, but he seems stronger now we are here, and there is more room, which we will need when Aunt has her baby. It will share our room, which will be useful when it is my turn to care for it.
>
> The day after we arrived there was a festival. The gamelan band played in the village and we had nasi goreng with chicken, as a special treat.
>
> Lots of people called, '*Selamat datang,*' which made us all feel good. Then father disappeared for hours to talk to the musicians. We have some instruments at school but father says playing is not for girls, so I can't learn.
>
> Next week is *Nyepi*, so it will be really quiet here then, but I do enjoy that as well. We are going to clean the gods we brought with us so they are prepared for the day. I don't have a job here yet, so I am helping at home more whilst I find someone in the market who would like a willing worker before school each day.

1 Give three ways the writer shows that the narrator is not in England. Support your answer with references to the text.

a) _____

_____

b) _____

_____

c) _____

_____

1

6 marks

2 What age is the writer? Support your answer with evidence from the text.

_____

_____

2

2 marks

3 Use evidence from the text to draw conclusions on how families live in where the text is set (Indonesia).

_____

_____

_____

_____

_____

_____

3

4 marks

4a

5 marks

4 a) List the words and phrases from the text that you would put into a glossary.

_____

_____

_____

4b

1 mark

b) Why is a glossary needed for these words and phrases? _____

_____

/18

Total for this test

> **At Level 6 pupils should know that:**
> - The level of formality in a piece of writing depends on its purpose, style and audience.

Formal or informal?

Formal and informal styles must be chosen to suit the purpose of the writing. Whilst one is not necessarily better than the other, there are situations where using one rather than the other is the correct choice to make. A letter to your best friend, for instance, would have a very different level of formality than one to your bank manager. It is generally better to be too formal than too informal.

Some features of an informal writing style

- the purpose of the text (think about the styles used for a letter of complaint, a letter to support a job application and a letter of condolence)
- the situation of the writer (constraints placed by the text and personal circumstances)
- cultural influences (the periodic sentence – a long sentence that has the main point at the end –was popular in classical times!)
- the need to avoid monotony.

Some features of a formal writing style

- complex and passive voice sentences are used
- objective (points are clearly stated and explained without undue emotion)
- punctuation is functional (exclamation marks are avoided)
- words are written in full (no contractions or abbreviations)
- the third person is used (not I, you, we or us).

In the classroom

Display a 'Formality Meter' (a horizontal line marked 'informal' at one end and 'formal' at the other, with a moveable marker on it).

↓

Have sticky notes with features of in/formal writing and have pupils stick them appropriately *above* the Formality Meter. Discuss and adjust as necessary.

↓

Give pupils sticky notes (preferably in a different colour) with different types of writing written on each (e.g. text message, business letter, police report, story, note to mum, a draft for your topic report, school report).

↓

Ask pupils to discuss where on the Formality Meter each type of writing should be placed.

↓

Discuss responses and place the sticky notes appropriately *below* the Formality Meter.

↓

Pupils can use the completed Formality Meter to match texts and features.

Sample answers (answers will vary)

1. A, G, D, E, B, F, C
2. a–d any of: complex sentences, passive voice sentences, objective, punctuation is functional, no contractions or abbreviations, the third person used
3. I, H, M, J, L, K
4. a) The telephone is out of order. b) Lani loves to argue. c) This food is not digestible. d) That's naughty.

1 Match these texts with the positions on the Formality Meter by writing the letter position next to the text.

A   B   C   D   E   F   G

| INFORMAL | FORMALITY METER | FORMAL |

_____ email to a friend about meeting up

_____ an application for a job

_____ a letter to an aunt, thanking her for a birthday present

_____ a police report about an accident

_____ a diary entry about a day at school

_____ a report about a science experiment

_____ a story about a fantasy world

| | 1 |

7 marks

2 List four features of formal writing.

a) _____

b) _____

c) _____

d) _____

| | 2 |

4 marks

3 Match these sentences with the positions on the Formality Meter by writing the letter position next to the sentence.

H   I   J   K   L   M

| INFORMAL | FORMALITY METER | FORMAL |

_____ Guess what I did yesterday.

_____ The biz – well cool!

_____ It is inappropriate to set such high standards for young children.

_____ Please, please may we have it here?

_____ The man, who was in his fifties, disappeared without trace.

_____ His eyes were pools of fear and uncertainty.

| | 3 |

6 marks

4 Complete the table to show formal and informal ways of writing each sentence.

Formal writing	Informal writing
I am unable to attend.	I can't come.
a)	The phone won't work.
b) Lani appreciates debate.	
c)	This food is making me sick.
d) Such behaviour is not appropriate.	

| | 4 |

4 marks

| | /21 |

Total for this test

> ### At Level 6 pupils should know that:
> - A well-structured piece of writing needs to be planned.

Why writing needs to be planned

When writing in a test situation, plans need to be made as very brief notes that are to the point. The aim of a plan is to ensure that:

- a piece of writing has a sound structure
- material is presented in a logical and effective order
- material is relevant to the purpose of the writing
- the intended audience has been considered
- the writing has cohesion.

A quick method of planning

A basic five-point plan can be adjusted to fit most types of writing. Using the same system for each piece of writing gives pupils a familiar routine to start every piece of writing. Pupils could use a spider diagram (five legs!) and then number the legs for the order of the text.

Examples of five-point plans

These would need tailoring to the particular piece of work but provide a basic outline, showing what could be included in each step of the plan:

Story	Biography
1. setting	**1.** birth
2. characters	**2.** childhood and adolescence
3. the first stage of the problem	**3.** run-up to the important events
4. the main action	**4.** important events
5. resoultion	**5.** life after (to death?)
Letter of complaint	**Persuasion**
1. the origin of complaint	**1.** introduction
2. associated problems	**2.** first persuasive point
3. the consequences	**3.** second persuasive point
4. how you tried to solve it	**4.** third persuasive point
5. what you expect them to do (and what will happen if they don't)	**5.** what response expected from reader

In the classroom

Give pupils plans for different types of writing. Some should be good plans but others should have errors, such as too many notes, full sentences, too many points, too few points, not enough information, information not specific to the piece of writing, irrelevant material, material repeated or sections in the wrong order.

Allow pupils to discuss and evaluate the plans in pairs.

Collect responses for each plan, discuss and agree on the elements of a good plan.

Ask pupils to complete a plan for a piece of writing related to current class work.

Compare the plans and discuss.

1 Cross out the unnecessary words in this plan for a report about playground equipment. You may wish to change some words.

> 1. this is a report about the need to re-equip the playground – because equipment too small, not enough
> 2. firstly, size of the equipment – too small for the older children, designed for infants – older children need more challenge
> 3. in addition, more children in the school now so we need more equipment – everyone will get a turn
> 4. furthermore, safety – some repairs are needed – screws missing, split wood, bits not allowed on, needs painting
> 5. we will help raise money and summary – why we need equipment, the main reasons, we are willing to raise money – why we should be supported

5 marks   1

2 Write the order for the paragraphs in this plan by writing the numbers in the boxes.

Order	Section content
	pollution
	lots of accidents
	thinking about the problem of too many cars
	overcrowded roads
	next steps if concerned

2 marks   2

3 Complete this spider diagram for a writing plan about the benefits of being in your class, and then number each leg in the order you think it should appear in the writing. Remember your writing will need an introduction and a conclusion.

The benefits of being in my class

3 marks   3

4 Write a plan for a piece of writing about why and how you should plan your work.

_____

_____

_____

_____

_____

_____

5 marks   4

/15

Total for this test

> ## At Level 6 pupils should know that:
>
> • The written style used is greatly influenced by the purpose and audience.

Factors that affect stylistic choices

The purpose and audience factors that influence the style of a piece of writing include:

- the purpose of the text
  - o instruct
  - o inform
  - o entertain
  - o explain
  - o persuade
- the audience
  - ➤ age
  - ➤ literary experience
  - ➤ literary knowledge
  - ➤ interests
  - ➤ motivation for reading
  - ➤ understanding of English

Stylistic features

The features that indicate the style of writing include:

- a piece of writing has a sound structure
- material is presented in a logical and effective order
- material is relevant to the purpose of the writing
- the intended audience has been considered
- the writing has cohesion.

In the classroom

Revise purpose and audience, then display these two texts.

TEXT 1: *A plane got into difficulties during landing today. Tenthrow Airport issued a statement confirming that the wheels of a Boeing 747, which was flying in from Japan, failed to descend as the plane landed on runway 2 …*

TEXT 2: *I've just had the most frightening experience of my life. We were about to land at Tenthrow, when the cabin crew started to get panicky and rush about. Then the pilot said we had a slight problem and that landing could be rather bumpy! We were told to adopt the brace position. Well, people were crying and screaming. I thought I was going to die …*

↓

Ask pupils to compare and discuss the texts. What are the similarities and differences?

↓

Discuss the audience and purpose of each text and how the style reflects this (news report: factual, unemotional, referring to official statements, formal); (letter to friend: informal, chatty, emotive).

↓

Ask pupils to work in pairs and write an account of the event as if they are the pilot submitting an official report.

↓

Compare responses and discuss. Revise stylistic features as necessary.

Sample answers (answers will vary)

For all questions: Correct viewpoint (1 mark); all important information translated to the new writer (1 mark); style fit to purpose of the writing (1 mark).

1. Dear Gran, It was the most dreadful carnival. It was absolutely pouring it down and everyone was huddling into doorways and peering through shop windows at us. Our school had a fruit basket float. I had to dress up as a banana, and then the rain made the yellow dye run down my face. I'm still yellow now! Luckily the judges thought it was face paint and we got first prize (plus all the other schools withdrew because of the rain).

2. a) Get your passport, credit card and driver's licence.
   b) Research different hotels on the Internet.
   c) Bookmark any sites you are interested in.
   d) Choose your hotel and work through the booking pages.

3. Words on the advert such as 'the envy of your neighbours', 'smart exterior', 'the engine operates well' attributed to Crazy Cars; features listed – six passengers, newest model, the PQ brand, snail's pace, buy now

1

Whaley Weekly

Whaley Bridge Carnival was a great success last week. The wet weather couldn't dampen the enthusiasm of the crowd and the parade was of the usual high standard. Buxworth School float won first prize in the schools' section, for its wonderful representation of a fruit basket.

Write about the Whaley Bridge Carnival in the form of a paragraph in a letter that a pupil at Buxworth School writes to her grandmother.

_____

_____

_____

_____

_____

1

3 marks

2

Frustration! Booking a hol should be fun. Managed to find a super hotel on the computer but then lost the site & had to start again. Went through all these booking pages, then needed my passport. By the time I found it the site had timed out and I had to start again. Then I needed my credit card – couldn't find it for ages. Started again. Then it was my driver's licence. Need a hol NOW!

Rewrite this diary entry as a set of instructions for booking a holiday online.

_____

_____

_____

_____

_____

2

3 marks

3 Use the text to design a poster for the PQ Zoso people carrier.

The Zoso is the latest effort of PQ to hit the family market. Its smart exterior may be the envy of the neighbours but its six passenger seats assume that all the children are on the miniature side and enjoy mild discomfort (which can become acute on long journeys). The engine operates well, provided you are not expecting to achieve any speed above a snail's pace when going uphill. Think carefully before you buy. Crazy Cars August edition

3

3 marks

/9

Total for this test

At Level 6 pupils should know that:
- Stories can be written in the first or third person

First person narrative

Features	Comments
Uses I and we	The reader is addressed directly, making it easy to relate to the character.
The narrator is usually the main character.	Only the thoughts and feelings of the main character are known. Others have to be introduced through dialogue.
The story is restricted to where the main character is and / or what they know.	
The character must be established as believable.	

Third person narrative

Features	Comments
Uses he, she and they	
The narrator is usually the writer.	Different characters can narrate through dialogue.
The writer can know everything about every character and situation.	
The writer chooses when knowledge is revealed to the reader; the reader can know more than the character.	Knowing more than the main character can add suspense – the character walks unknowingly into danger.
The writer can comment on the story and characters.	The writer may be biased towards a character.
The characters must be established as believable and trustworthy.	

In the classroom

Read an extract from a story written in the first person and one from a story in the third person.

↓

Discuss pupil responses and preferences.

↓

Look at some books that pupils enjoy reading. Are they written in the third or first person?

↓

Ask pupils to work with a partner and list advantages and disadvantages of each style.

↓

Ask pupils to present a well-known story from two viewpoints (e.g. Cinderella from the point of view of one of the sisters and of the fairy godmother).

↓

Discuss how and why the versions vary.

↓

Discuss the implications of this for story writing.

Sample answers (answers will vary)

1. **a)** I, we **b)** he, she, they
2. 1 mark for reactions / feelings supported by elements of the situation, up to 3. **a)** teacher: disappointed that his pupils behaved badly; irritated that his lunch is interrupted **b)** child: upset he's fallen out with friend; angry that friend hit him; unfair that he is in trouble; apprehensive about what teacher will say / do; worried that mum will find out

    c) 1 mark per point to a maximum of 3. the characters see things from their own viewpoint, focus on what is important to them and their previous experiences in similar situations
3. 1 mark for reactions / feelings supported by elements of the situation, up to 3. **a)** She is sulky and won't join in, rude as she ignores her friend, thoughtless when she falls behind so the instructor has to go back **b)** He is selfish and focused on having his own good time, unobservant as he doesn't notice Sian is in pain.

    c) 1 mark per point, up to 2. First extract is seen through Charlie's eyes, no other source of information; second extract narrator explains what has happened so we feel sorry for Sian.

1 a) First person narrative uses _____

   b) Third person narrative uses _____

2 Two children are taken to see their teacher following a dispute at lunchtime. The teacher is in the staffroom eating his dinner. Write about this situation from the viewpoint of:

   a) the teacher _____

   _____

   _____

   b) one of the children _____

   _____

   _____

   c) Explain why the accounts are different _____

   _____

   _____

3 Read this account of a day out.

> I had a brilliant time gorge walking. We started with a jump off a huge rock – it was fantastic. Then we swam through gorges, slid into rockpools and climbed through waterfalls. Sian was a pain though. She seemed really keen to begin with, but then she got all sulky and moody and wouldn't join in with the rest of us. I kept trying to get her to join back in. We were way in front and the instructor had to go back and help her to catch up.

   a) What does the extract show us about Sian's character? _____

   _____

   _____

   Now read this account of the day out.

> Charlie loved the gorge walking but Sian didn't have such a good time. She cracked her foot against a hidden rock on the first jump and this had rather dampened her enthusiasm. Charlie kept calling, 'Come on, Sian!' but she was cautious, not wanting to hurt herself again. She ended up way back behind the group, limping on the bad foot and struggling to catch up, until the instructor went and helped her.

   b) Looking at the two extracts, what do we know about Charlie's character?

   _____

   _____

   c) Why do the two extracts create such a different impression?

   _____

   _____

   _____

Features used to create tension

Words: use emotive words to create an atmosphere (e.g. terrifying, horrific, stormy).

Information: convey through dialogue and action, so blocks of description don't stall the story, for example:
'It's over,' she said as the crane lifted its load.

Sentences varied: short sentences increase the pace, while long sentences relax it. Alternating between sections of tension and relief creates greater tension.

Empathy with the heroes: make the danger they face believable, with catastrophic consequences for the character (e.g. death or death of a loved one); give them insurmountable odds (e.g. *only one hour before the bomb detonates and I'm chained into a cage*); give them dilemmas to solve (e.g. *which child shall I save?*).

Unexpected events: give the reader information about what the villain is planning (that the hero doesn't know about) but then don't follow reader expectations. Make something unexpected happen (e.g. *the car blew up but the driver had jumped onto the back of a passing bin lorry*).

Postpone the action: put inconsequential sentences between sentences as you work towards the climax point (e.g. *He waited, petrified. The clock ticked, uncaring, in the hall. The click of a door. Sweat ran down his back in cold rivulets. Footsteps. Closer. The moonlight broke through the clouds, illuminated his dusty footprints*).

The first letter of each of these steps can be used to spell out **WISE UP**.

In the classroom

Ask pupils for ways of creating tension. Discuss and note responses.

Display **WISE UP** written vertically in capital letters. Use the features pupils have given to start to fill in the mnemonic. Support pupils in discussion as the rest of the mnemonic is completed.

Work through each step, asking pupils to write examples that demonstrate the use of each feature.

Share completed examples and discuss responses.

Give pupils the opportunity to work with a partner to complete an extended piece of writing showing a build up of tension.

Sample answers (answers will vary)

1. aberration, recalcitrant, fiendishness, impetuosity, frenetic, intransigent
2. A car drove past, the driver only having to think about home and comfort. In the distance a dog barked, probably at an innocent walker. My hands were barely shaking this time, I noticed with satisfaction.
3. 1 mark if the response is suitable, 1 mark if it is original. **a)** Someone drops a rope ladder over the wall; she climbs through a man-hole, too small for the thugs to fit through. **b)** The parachute snags on the top of a very tall tree; a helicopter swoops down and rescues him; he falls into a deep, hidden mountain lake. **c)** He is an Olympic gymnast and vaults over to grab a knife from the table; he is wearing special protective clothing that cannot be pierced; police are hidden in the room.
4. 1 mark if the response is suitable, 1 mark if it is original. **a)** her husband will find out she took it from the bank and kill her. **b)** everyone will leave the remote desert base, the air conditioning will go off and he will die – slowly.

1 Use a dictionary to find and write six emotive words that you don't know the meaning of, which you can use in a story where tension is built.

a) word _____ meaning _____

_____

b) word _____ meaning _____

_____

c) word _____ meaning _____

_____

d) word _____ meaning _____

_____

e) word _____ meaning _____

_____

f) word _____ meaning _____

_____

	1
6 marks	

2 Postpone the action by putting other information between these sentences.

The lights went out. So he was here. I tensed. _____ .

Slowly, I took position. _____ I aimed

my gun, finger poised on the trigger. _____

_____ Crack! The blow from behind struck without warning.

	2
3 marks	

3 Write an unexpected next step for each situation.
a) The heroine is at the end of a cul-de-sac and is facing three enormous thugs.

_____

_____

_____

	3a
2 marks	

b) The hero is falling to the ground and his parachute has had enormous holes cut in it.

_____

_____

_____

	3b
2 marks	

c) The weaponless hero is facing the villain, who is wielding a long, sharp sword.

_____

_____

_____

	3c
2 marks	

4 Give original reasons why these heroes have these time constraints.
a) She has one hour to retrieve the stolen diamond because _____

_____

_____

	4a
2 marks	

b) He has ten minutes to get out of the locked room because _____

_____

_____

	4b
2 marks	

	/19
Total for this test	

Phrases

Phrases may have a noun or verb or both, but do not have a subject doing the verb. For example:

swimming with strength and confidence

Independent clauses

Independent clauses have a subject doing a verb and could stand alone as a sentence. For example:

the house looked derelict

Dependent clauses (or subordinate clauses)

Dependent clauses have a subject doing a verb and start with a subordinate conjunction. They cannot stand alone as a sentence. Some common subordinate conjunctions:

> after, although, if, unless, as, until, when, as soon as, because, whenever

For example: *whenever it was raining*

Combining dependent and independent clauses

a) If a sentence starts with a dependent clause, a comma is needed before the independent clause. For example: *Although the sun was hot, the boy went running.*

b) If a sentence starts with an independent clause, a comma is not required before the dependent clause. For example: *The boy went running although the sun was hot.*

c) If a sentence has a dependent clause in the middle, it has a comma before and after. For example: *The boy, although the sun was hot, went running.*

In the classroom

Give pupils a mixture of phrases, independent clauses and dependent clauses. Explain that you want them to read each group of words and group them according to structure. Collect results and discuss.

If pupils show a clear understanding, move on to another topic. If not, skip the next step.

Ask them to underline the verbs in one colour and the subjects in the other.

Make two piles: one where the subject is doing the verb and the other where it isn't.

Explain that the first pile is clauses and the other is phrases.

Split the first pile into complete sentences and incomplete sentences.

Explain that the first pile is dependent clauses and the other is independent clauses.

Sample answers (answers will vary)

1.

	Independent clause	Dependent clause	Phrase
a) the fox jumped	✓		
b) whilst the radio was on		✓	
c) during the football match			✓
d) after we ate dinner		✓	
e) a large, fierce dog			✓
f) the fire crackled	✓		
g) running swiftly and silently			✓

2. a) Despite her lack of revision, <u>she passed the test</u>.
   b) The rain poured all day so <u>we ended up soaked</u>.
   c) <u>The chess tournament</u>, after a slow start, <u>was won by Max</u>.
   d) Although Amir ran as fast as he could, <u>Barti overtook him</u>.
   e) <u>Immi</u>, who normally loved pasta, <u>refused to eat the spaghetti</u>.
   f) <u>The tractor turned off</u>, even though the road looked wider up ahead.

3. a) people on the departing train b) watched the seagulls as they landed c) the confused and unhappy toddler d) creaking and groaning in an alarming way e) after the weather forecast f) banged and scraped against the coins

4. 1 mark for rewriting, 1 mark for convincing reason.
   a) ii) I wanted to go out for a ride instead whenever I had to work. ii) i) because it emphasises that I had to work. / ii) because it emphasises what I really wanted to do. b) ii) Even though she was unwell, the singer still performed. iii) i) because it shows it was important that the singer performed / ii) because it draws attention to the fact that she was ill. c) ii) Immediately after the rain had stopped, the animals gathered at the waterhole. iii) ii) because it shows that the action happened straight away. iii) because it shows it was raining.

1 Complete the table.

	Independent clause	Dependent clause	Phrase
a) the fox jumped			
b) whilst the radio was on			
c) during the football match			
d) after we ate dinner			
e) a large, fierce dog			
f) the fire crackled			
g) running swiftly and silently			

7 marks   1

2 Underline the independent clause in each sentence and add any necessary punctuation.

a) Despite her lack of revision she passed the test.

b) The rain poured all day so we ended up soaked.

c) The chess tournament after a slow start was won by Max.

d) Although Amir ran as fast as he could Barti overtook him.

e) Immi who normally loved pasta refused to eat the spaghetti.

f) The tractor turned off even though the road looked wider up ahead.

6 marks   2

3 Insert a phrase with at least four words in it on each line.

a) The _____ waved enthusiastically.

b) The two men _____ on the cliff.

c) Walking unsteadily, _____ made his way through the town.

d) _____ the car climbed the hill.

e) Look at the cloudless sky _____ said it would rain.

f) The phone _____ in my pocket.

6 marks   3

4 Rewrite these sentences, changing the order of the dependent and the independent clauses. Remember to punctuate the new sentence correctly. For each pair of sentences put an asterisk next to the sentence you think is more effective and explain why you think that.

a) i) Whenever I had to work, I wanted to go out for a ride instead.

ii) _____

iii) I think _____ is more effective because _____

_____

4a   2 marks

b) i) The singer still performed even though she was unwell.

ii) _____

iii) I think _____ is more effective because _____

_____

4b   2 marks

c) i) The animals gathered at the waterhole immediately after the rain had stopped.

ii) _____

iii) I think _____ is more effective because _____

_____

4c   2 marks

/25

Total for this test

> **At Level 6 pupils should know that:**
> - Clarity in sentences is essential to ensure that communication is effective.
> - Correct punctuation, effective word choices and considered word order all promote clarity.

Some features that improve clarity

Punctuating correctly: Consider the meaning of these two sentences:

> *The children who were behaving badly had to stay in.*
> *The children, who were behaving badly, had to stay in.*

Ordering words intelligently: Consider the meaning of these two sentences:

> *The man took the car in the garage.*
> *The man in the garage took the car.*

Considering the effects of word choice: Consider the meaning of this sentence:

> *I went swimming in my car.*
> (So was the car full of water or did I take my car in the pool?)

Using pronouns clearly: Consider the meaning of this sentence:

> *He took the cat in the basket and when he got home he put it in the loft so he would know where it was.*

Using active sentences: Remember that active sentences are easier to understand than passive sentences.

> *The van was chased by the police car.* (passive)
> *The police car chased the van.* (active)

Using connectives: to signal sentence links to the reader.

In the classroom

> Display the example sentences given in the first column and give pupils individual copies.

⬇

> In pairs, ask pupils to read through the sentences and discuss the meanings of each one. Tell them to make a note of any sentences that are difficult to understand.

⬇

> Discuss responses.

⬇

> Look at each sentence in turn, questioning what the sentences actually mean and whether this was what the writer actually intended.

⬇

> Ask pupils to find ways to rewrite the sentences that will make the meanings clear.

⬇

> Collect responses and discuss any differences.

Sample answers (answers will vary)

1. a) Sounds like the pots were in the man's pyjamas; The man washed the pots whilst wearing his pyjamas. b) You can't tell which girl was speaking; Stephanie showed Caitlin her work and explained that she needed to get some help because she didn't think it was very good. c) Sounds like the neighbour likes to eat carrots; When Mark was away, a neighbour fed the donkey carrots. d) It isn't clear whether you soak the baby or the nappy; If a baby soils a cloth nappy, soak the nappy in bleach. e) It isn't clear whether we were told at 6am or whether the coach would leave at 6am; We were told the coach would leave at 6am.
2. a) i) Only the tame monkeys let the children hold them. ii) All the monkeys were tame and held by the children. b) i) Only the cakes which had gone stale were thrown away. ii) All the cakes were stale and had to be thrown away. c) i) The boy in the park now plays the drums. ii) The boy took drums to the park and played there. d) i) That horse in the field ate the carrots. ii) The horse ate the carrots which were in the field.

1 Explain what makes the following sentences difficult to understand, then rewrite each sentence making your meaning clear.

a) The man washed the pots in his pyjamas.

Difficulty: _____

Rewriting: _____

> 1a
>
> 2 marks

b) Stephanie showed Caitlin her work and she said she needed to get some help because she didn't think it was very good.

Difficulty: _____

Rewriting: _____

> 1b
>
> 2 marks

c) The donkey was given his dinner by a neighbour who liked carrots.

Difficulty: _____

Rewriting: _____

> 1c
>
> 2 marks

d) If a baby soils a cloth nappy, soak it in bleach.

Difficulty: _____

Rewriting: _____

> 1d
>
> 2 marks

e) We were told at 6am the coach would leave.

Difficulty: _____

Rewriting: _____

> 1e
>
> 2 marks

2 Explain the meaning of each of these sentences.

a) i) The monkeys which were tame let the children hold them. _____

_____

   ii) The monkeys, which were tame, let the children hold them. _____

_____

> 2a
>
> 2 marks

b) i) The cakes which were stale had to be thrown away. _____

_____

   ii) The cakes, which were stale, had to be thrown away. _____

_____

> 2b
>
> 2 marks

c) i) The boy in the park played the drums. _____

_____

   ii) The boy played the drums in the park. _____

_____

> 2c
>
> 2 marks

c) i) The horse in the field ate the carrots. _____

_____

> 2d
>
> 2 marks

   ii) The horse ate the carrots in the field. _____

_____

> /18
>
> Total for this test

At Level 6 pupils should know that:

- A good opening sentence makes a reader want to read on.
- Good opening sentences shock, surprise, raise questions or arouse curiosity.

Opening sentences

Opening sentences set the tone of the story. The writer needs to capture the readers so that they will continue to read. Short and simple sentences work well as they are quickly processed, but within them must be an element that will shock, surprise, raise questions or arouse curiosity.

Opening sentences come in many different forms, but some strategies to consider are using:

- dialogue so the reader immediately engages with the characters, for example:

    'You get back in here right now,' shouted Aunty Pat.

- a description that leaves the reader wanting to know more, for example:

    The green-skinned people had the bluest hair I had ever seen.

- a dramatic event that shocks the reader, for example:

    Tearing back the paper, Tom saw the face of a dead man.

- setting the tone, such as action packed, mysterious, lazy, for example:

    The man slipped out like a wisp of smoke through a crack in the wall.

In the classroom

Discuss the job of an opening sentence. Do not accept the general answer, 'To hook the reader'. Pupils need to be explaining exactly how that is done.

Collect a variety of opening sentences from books in school and / or books that the children bring in. Emphasise that different things appeal to different readers and that not all readers enjoy the same books. Pass around cards with opening sentences written on them and ask pupils to read and mark them 1, 2 or 3 depending on their level of interest.

Discuss the differences in the responses.

Ask pupils to sort the sentences into the types of opening and let pupils decide on a classification for each group (questions, dialogue …).

Ask pupils to find ways to rewrite the sentences that will make the meanings clear.

Discuss the responses and whether there are any other types of opening that could be added.

Sample answers (answers will vary)

1.

Story	A question	To shock	Characterisation
Three Little Pigs	What hope is there for homeless pigs?	Death by boiling seemed inevitable.	'He started it!' cried Ben.
Goldilocks	What would you do if you found a strange house?	Without a thought, he shot the intruder.	'Why is it always porridge?' wondered Goldilocks.
Cinderella	Aren't sisters the absolute limit?	Slavery is underrated today.	'Trained mice are the future,' decided Cinderella.
Little Red Riding Hood	Who would want to wear a red cloak?	The wolf pounced with a snarl.	'Come and get me!' she called.

2. **a)** The storm blew the car over the cliff. **b)** As the house burned, I saw the silhouette of a cat in an upstairs window. **c)** 'Give me the bike,' ordered the knife-wielding youth. **d)** Ice cream on your face isn't the best way to end a fight.

3. 1 mark each for relevance, originality and style. Check pupil answers for relevance, originality, and style.

1   Complete the table by writing different opening sentences for these well-known stories.

Story	A question	To shock	Characterisation
Three Little Pigs			
Goldilocks			
Cinderella			
Little Red Riding Hood			

<table>
<tr><td>12 marks</td><td>1</td></tr>
</table>

2   Write an opening sentence combing these subjects and objects.

a) a storm and a car

b) a house and a cat

c) a boy and a bike

d) an ice cream and a fight

<table>
<tr><td>4 marks</td><td>2</td></tr>
</table>

3   Write a paragraph following on from these opening sentences.

a) The box on the doorstep rocked slightly as I reached towards it.

_____

_____

_____

_____

<table>
<tr><td>3 marks</td><td>3a</td></tr>
</table>

b) The man was dead. I was alone.

_____

_____

_____

_____

<table>
<tr><td>3 marks</td><td>3b</td></tr>
</table>

c) Why was *he* here?

_____

_____

_____

_____

<table>
<tr><td>3 marks</td><td>3c</td></tr>
</table>

/25

Total for this test

At Level 6 pupils should know that:

- Concise writing uses technically accurate words.
- Content should not be repeated unless it is for emphasis or effect.
- Only relevant material should be included in the text.

Concision

When writing for concision, material needs to be carefully selected and focused on the topic. Concise writing will display these features:

- only relevant material included
- no needless repetition of individual words
- no needless repetition of information
- long, drawn-out explanations are avoided
- technical words are used appropriately to replace longer descriptions.

Word choices and order need to be accurate, economical and effective, with the use of appropriate technical vocabulary. Concise writing is essential in many forms of non-fiction writing, such as instructions, adverts and letters of application and complaint.

In the classroom

Display the sentence:
> *Olives grow on trees and olive trees grow in hot countries where the sun makes the fruit ripen around September so that is when they collect all the olives from the trees.*

↓

Ask pupils to read, copy and then discuss the effectiveness of the sentence.

↓

With partners, ask pupils to suggest ways in which the sentence could be made more effective.

↓

Collect ideas and discuss.

↓

Ask pupils to underline the key words in the sentence ('olive trees', 'hot countries', 'ripe', 'September', 'collect').

↓

Challenge pairs to make a more concise sentence, maybe changing some phrases to technical words.
> *Olive trees thrive in Mediterranean countries and the olives are harvested in September.*

↓

Repeat the exercise with different sentences.

Sample answers (answers will vary)

1. **a)** lawnmower **b)** pliers **c)** clock / stopwatch / watch **d)** protractor **e)** germination **f)** physicist
2. 1 for correct underlining; 1 mark for a fair attempt and 2 marks for a good answer.
   <u>holidays</u>, <u>Joshua</u>, <u>all</u> <u>his</u> <u>time</u>, <u>farm</u>, <u>help</u>, <u>enjoys</u>
   In the holidays Joshua likes to help his dad on the farm by looking after the cows, keeping the dairy clean, bailing hay and driving the tractor.
3. 2 marks each – allow 1 mark for a fair attempt. **a)** The van was too large to negotiate the narrow street. **b)** The leak in the flat is damaging my property and causing a problem with damp. **c)** This toothpaste removes plaque, whitens teeth and makes your breath smell fresh. **d)** With a few chords, you can play many well-known songs on the guitar. **e)** When you receive money, put it in an interest-earning account.

1 Replace these groups of words with one word that means the same thing.

a) a machine that you use to cut the grass _____

b) a tool used to pull nails out of wood _____

c) a device for measuring time _____

d) something used to measure angles _____

e) the stage in a plant lifecycle when the seed starts to grow _____

f) a person who studies forces and how things move _____

	1

6 marks

2 Underline the key words in this sentence and then write a more concise version.

> In the holidays Joshua spends all his time doing things on the farm like milking the cows and bailing the hay and checking the herd and cleaning the dairy and driving the tractor because he likes to help his dad and he is very good at doing things on the farm and he enjoys it more than anything else.

_____

_____

_____

	2

3 marks

3 Write a more concise version of these sentences.

a) The big van was very large so it couldn't fit down the narrow street because the houses, flats and offices were too close together so it couldn't get through.

_____

_____

	3a

2 marks

b) The flat I rent has a leak and the water gets in and makes my clothes wet and other things so I have to clean them and it's making the carpet damp so it smells as well.

_____

_____

	3b

2 marks

c) This toothpaste can get your teeth really clean because it removes all the stuff that sticks to your teeth so your teeth look really white and it has a good smell so your breath smells fresh after you have used it.

_____

_____

	3c

2 marks

d) The guitar is a great instrument to play because with a few different notes put together you can play lots of different songs which are written by lots of different writers and you don't need to learn loads of notes before you can play songs that all your friends will know.

_____

_____

	3d

2 marks

e) If you get money for doing jobs, on special occasions, or for your birthday, it is a good idea to put it in a bank or building society or the post office or something like that so that you get more money and you can save it for something special and it will be worth more money than it was when you put it in.

_____

_____

	3e

2 marks

	/19

Total for this test

At Level 6 pupils should know that:

- Connectives link ideas within a sentence, between sentences and between paragraphs.
- Connectives should be carefully chosen to suit their purpose.

Important connective groups

(with examples)

Change of focus / topic	Cause and effect	Giving examples
turning to	therefore	for instance
as regards	so	such as
concerning	as a result of	as can be seen by
moving on to	because	as is shown by
now to consider	due to this	take the case of

Concessions	Summing up	Emphasising
although	in conclusion	not only
whilst it is true	in summary	mainly
despite the fact	to conclude	mostly
despite this	to round off	unfortunately
nevertheless	overall	

Listing points	Contrasting	Rephrasing
firstly, secondly	however	in other words
to begin with	on the other hand	to put it more
as well	although	simply
on top of this	whereas	
in addition	on the contrary	
more importantly		

Comparison
compared with
in comparison
likewise
similarly
equally

In the classroom

Give all the connectives (plus any others) on cards. Ask pupils to sort them into groups.

Ask pupils to define the groups they have made.

Discuss how the connectives and connective groups could be used in writing.

Look at some examples of non-fiction writing. Highlight the connectives and group them.

Discuss which groups are prevalent in different pieces of writing and why. (It will be greatly influenced by the style and purpose of the text.)

Repeat the exercise with fiction texts.

Ask pupils to write sentences connected with specific connectives so they become familiar with usage. Emphasise that a connective is not necessarily a conjunction, so separate sentences will usually be needed.

Sample answers (answers will vary)

1. blue for cause and effect (2 marks) – <u>due to</u>, <u>so that</u>, <u>became</u>; red for contrasting (1 mark) – <u>although</u>; green for examples (1 mark) – <u>as can be seen by</u>

2. a) went out even though it was snowing and didn't really want to b) went out every time it snowed c) went out if the snow was falling d) went out because it was snowing

3. a) as an extra point b) disapproving, stopping something else happening c) the whole purpose of text was to prove this point d) to make sure the main message is clear and understood

4. a) Contrary to popular opinion, school can be enormous fun. b) You will not be allowed out at playtime. Furthermore, you will have to write a letter of apology. c) The experiment was a success so, consequently, we will be installing this equipment in every classroom. d) His skills are improving, as is shown by his improved time. e) I told you it was forbidden. Nevertheless, you chose to attend the meeting. f) The house was immaculate. In comparison, the garden was a tip.

5. a) despite b) This resulted c) the cause d) however e) resulting in f) despite

1 Underline the connectives in this paragraph. Use blue for cause and effect connectives, red for contrasting and green for examples.

> Although we enjoyed our holiday, the journey was very disappointing. Due to a flight delay, we had trouble getting into our accommodation, so that our youngest child became greatly distressed, as can be seen by the enclosed photograph.

	1
	4 marks

2 Explain the meaning of the sentence when these connectives are used to fill the gap.

_____ it was snowing, I went out.

a) although _____

b) whenever _____

c) whilst _____

d) due to the fact that _____

	2
	4 marks

3 Explain the meaning of the sentence when these connectives are used to fill the gap.

_____ , the school day finishes too late.

a) in addition _____

b) unfortunately _____

c) in conclusion _____

d) to clarify the point _____

	3
	4 marks

4 Write one or two sentences to show a good use of each connective.

a) contrary to _____

_____

b) furthermore _____

_____

c) consequently _____

_____

d) as is shown by _____

_____

e) nevertheless _____

_____

f) in comparison _____

_____

	4
	6 marks

5 Fill in the gaps with appropriate connectives.

a) _____ arriving very late, James was collected from the station by Aiden.

b) _____ in them both going to bed after midnight and c) _____ of much bad temper the following day. d) _____ , everyone was understanding

e) _____ a positive experience for all, f) _____ the difficult start.

	5
	6 marks

	/24
	Total for this test

> **At Level 6 pupils should know that:**
> * Combining sentences gives clarity and avoids repetition.
> * Combined sentences should be closely related

Steps to sentence combining

Look for words that can be changed into adjectives:

> *bought a cake from the shop* becomes *a shop-bought cake*

Use modifying clauses (but make sure they are placed close to the words they modify). Modifying clauses give more information or clarify meaning and are based on adjectives and adverbs. They often give information about how, when and where:

> *The man, **who was very tiresome**, kept phoning me **whilst** I was at work.*

Delete repeated and unnecessary words:

> *The guitar was shiny, like it was ~~a new guitar.~~*

Avoid using co-ordinating conjunctions as much as possible as they join rather than combine sentences. The co-ordinating conjunctions are: for, and, nor, but, or, yet, so. (Remember them using **FANBOYS**.)

Example

The toddler wanted the orange dish. The toddler's mother was looking harassed and refused to give it to him. He started to scream. He was a determined young man and strong enough to cry for a very long time. He cried for three hours!

The strong, determined toddler screamed unceasingly for three hours when his harassed-looking mother wouldn't give him the orange dish.

In the classroom

> Give pupils two simple sentences that are related in meaning (such as, *I bought a cake. It was tasty*).

> Ask pupils how they could combine the sentences without using the word 'and'.

> Compare responses and discuss any differences. (*I bought a tasty cake. / The cake I bought was tasty. I bought a cake which was tasty. It was tasty, the cake I bought.*)

> Repeat with other pairs of related sentences, then extend to more than two sentences but always combining all the information into just one sentence.

> Challenge pupils to make the shortest sentence they can by combining all the information.

Sample answers (answers will vary)

1. **a)** The terrified rabbit disappeared into the hedge. **b)** My new house is on the main road. **c)** Someone needs to turn down the loud music that is keeping me awake. **d)** 1 mark for combining two sentences, 2 marks for all. Tomorrow I am going to watch the cup-final match in Manchester. **e)** 1 mark for combining two sentences, 2 marks for all. My Grade 4 clarinet exam this afternoon, for which I have spent months preparing, is making me feel very nervous. **f)** 1 mark for combining two sentences, 2 marks for all. On my birthday, my friend made me a delicious lemon cake topped with orange and yellow jelly sweets.

2. **a) i)** The puppy was playful. **ii)** It bit me. **b) i)** The train was small. **ii)** It was just a local train. **iii)** It went through the station. **iv)** It didn't stop. **c) i)** The boy was angry. **ii)** He had been saving for weeks. **iii)** He wanted an Electronic Atom Whip. **iv)** He saw someone buy one. **v)** It was the last one. **vi)** He felt very frustrated.

3. avoids repetition; adds clarity; makes writing more concise; cuts out lots of small, choppy sentences

1 Combine each group of sentences into one sentence. Make your sentence concise.

a) The rabbit was terrified. It disappeared into the hedge.

_____

	1a
	1 mark

b) The road is a main road. I am moving to a new house. My new house is on that road.

_____

	1b
	1 mark

c) The music is keeping me awake. It is very loud. Someone needs to turn it down.

_____

_____

	1c
	1 mark

d) The match is tomorrow. It is the cup-final. It is being played in Manchester. I am going to watch it.

_____

_____

	1d
	2 marks

e) I play the clarinet. I've got an exam this afternoon. It is my Grade 4. I have been practising my pieces for months. I feel very nervous.

_____

_____

_____

	1e
	2 marks

f) It was my birthday. My friend made me a cake. It was a lemon cake. It had orange and yellow jelly sweets on top. It was absolutely delicious.

_____

_____

_____

	1f
	2 marks

2 Write the sentences that were combined to make these sentences.

a) The playful puppy bit me.   i) _____

                         ii) _____

	2a
	1 mark

b) The small local train went through the station without stopping.

i) _____

ii) _____

iii) _____

iv) _____

	2b
	2 marks

c) The angry, frustrated boy, who had been saving for weeks, saw someone buy the last Electronic Atom Whip in the shop.

i) _____

ii) _____

iii) _____

iv) _____

v) _____

vi) _____

	2c
	3 marks

	3
	2 marks

3 Give two advantages of combining sentences.

a) _____

b) _____

	/17
	Total for this test

Verbs

Verbs are one of the most important word classes. They are words for actions and states of being (existence) and every sentence needs a verb. More unusual verbs are interesting for the reader, and good writers make good verb choices.

Verbs can suggest different intensities and writers need to consider when to use forceful and powerful verbs, and when to select those that are gentler. Consider these choices for the verb 'run':

jog, stride, sprint, dash, bolt, flee, canter, lope, race

Although they all denote running, they create very different images. The art of good writing is selecting the most appropriate verb for the purpose.

Adverbs

Adverbs modify verbs and give further information. Placing the adverb in different places in the sentence can create different shades of meaning by changing the emphasis.

Consider these positions:
- after the action
  Rowan moved his hand suddenly and caught my arm.
- before the action
  Rowan suddenly moved his hand and caught my arm.
- at the start of the sentence
  Suddenly, Rowan moved his hand and caught my arm.

In the classroom

List some frequently used verbs (run, walk, look, say, got, had, put …) and give pupils a limited time (about 3 minutes) to list as many interesting alternatives to these words as possible.

Collect and discuss the results.

Give pupils dictionaries and thesauri and challenge them to find more unusual alternatives.

Ask pupils to use less familiar verbs in constructing sentences, first orally with a partner, and then written.

Discuss the role of adverbs in these sentences.

Try placing adverbs in different positions in the sentences and discuss the effects.

Sample answers (answers will vary)

1. a) slid b) purchased c) completed d) perceived e) promenaded f) baked
2. b) regularly c) faintly d) uproariously e) strangely f) effortlessly (positioning should vary)
3. a) The spy divulged the secret. b) She interceded for the thief. c) The runner began to dehydrate. d) The sailor had to tighten the rope. e) The teacher exonerated the boy.
4. a) places the emphasis on it being Max who moved slowly b) places the emphasis on Max answering the question
   c) places the emphasis on the hand lifting slowly

1 Use synonyms for the verbs in these sentences to create clearer images.

a) He put the paper into his briefcase.

_____

b) We got some food at the restaurant.

_____

c) We did a lot of work at school.

_____

d) She saw a menacing shadow.

_____

e) He walked down the road.

_____

f) We made a cake.

_____

	1
	6 marks

2 Add an adverb to each sentence. Insert it with an arrow, deciding whether it should go at the start of the sentence, before the verb or after the verb. The first one has been done for you.

Devastatingly,

a) ↓The river raged through the valley.

b) The dog menaced the postman.

c) Despite the pain, the man only groaned.

d) When we saw the parcel, we all laughed.

e) In the snow, the village appeared beautiful.

f) The dancer glided across the stage.

	2
	6 marks

3 Write a sentence using each verb correctly. If necessary, check the meaning in a dictionary.

a) divulge

_____

b) intercede

_____

c) dehydrate

_____

d) tauten

_____

e) exonerate

_____

	3
	5 marks

4 Describe the effect of the position of the adverb in these sentences.

a) Max slowly lifted his hand to answer the question.

	4
	3 marks

b) Slowly, Max lifted his hand to answer the question.

c) Max lifted his hand slowly to answer the question.

	/20
	Total for this test

At Level 6 pupils should know that:

- Similes, metaphors and personification are types of figurative language that help writers convey clear images.
- Metaphors are more powerful than similes.

Similes

Similes compare one thing to another and can usually be identified by the word pattern 'as … as a ….' or the word 'like'. Many similes are well known, but it is more effective to create original similes:

> *as white as snow*
> *as high as a kite*
> *like a bat out of hell*
> *The cave was like an open mouth ready to swallow unwary travellers.*

Metaphors

Metaphors state that one thing is like another that displays the characteristics the writer wants to convey:

> *The sea was a hungry monster clawing at the cliffs.*

Personification

Personification is a type of metaphor that makes objects sound human:

> *The trees reached with gnarled hands and tangled in his hair.*

In the classroom

Activity 1 – similes / metaphors

Ask pupils what similes and metaphors are and why they are used.

↓

List as many well-known similes as possible and discuss making new similes.

↓

Give pupils a set of sentence openers such as:
He walked … She watched … They listened … Her bag was … and a set of pictures of objects (mouse, stone, car, flower …).

↓

Tell pupils to take a card and a sentence opener and combine the two in a sentence using a simile (results can be very funny!). The activity also works with metaphors.

Activity 2 – personification

Ask pupils what personification is and why it is used.

↓

Give pupils a set of pictures of objects (stone, car, flower …).

↓

Challenge pupils to personify each object.

Sample answers (answers will vary)

1. **a)** The house was an oven. **b)** The river was like a sleepy snake. **c)** The sun was a golden coin. **d)** The boat was like a bobbing cork. **e)** The man was like a raging beast.

2.

	Simile	Metaphor	Personification
a) as light as a feather	✓		
b) the sun stroked her hair			✓
c) the water beckoned the hot boy			✓
d) the fog was a grey blanket		✓	
e) cry like a baby	✓		
f) the rain was a shower of needles		✓	

3. **a)** deep space **b)** an orbiting satellite **c)** nylon cable **d)** carefree child **e)** a model **f)** an Olympic gold medallist

4. 1 mark for two underlined, 2 marks for all **a)** car flushed, roared with frustration, pushing every last bit of energy into its wheels, sighed with relief **b)** they are personification

5. **a)** 1 mark each – provided the content is different.

	Simile	Metaphor	Personification
car	as old as the planet	was a roaring dragon	grumbled
tower crane	like a giraffe	was a needle	sighed
bag	as heavy as a kettlebell	was a cavern	yawned

b) i) The car was a roaring dragon raging through the city streets looking for a victim. **ii)** The tower crane was a needle piercing through the ruins and smog to the sky. **iii)** The bag was a huge cavern that made it impossible to locate any specific item.

1 Complete the table by converting the similes and metaphors.
The first one has been done for you.

Simile	Metaphor
His fur was like pure silk.	*His fur was pure silk.*
a) The house was like an oven	
b)	The river was a sleepy snake.
c) The sun was like a golden coin.	
d)	The boat was a bobbing cork.
e)	The man was a raging beast.

1
5 marks

2 Complete the table.

	Simile	Metaphor	Personification
a) as light as a feather			
b) the sun stroked her hair			
c) the water beckoned the hot boy			
d) the fog was a grey blanket			
e) cry like a baby			
f) the rain was a shower of needles			

2
6 marks

3 Finish these similes as originally as possible.

a) as black as _____   b) as high as _____   c) as strong as _____

d) whistle like a _____   e) as thin as _____   f) run like a _____

3
6 marks

4 a) Underline the metaphors in the passage.

> The car flushed with rage. It roared with frustration as the hill got ever steeper.
> Pushing every last bit of energy into its wheels, it screeched over the brow and
> sighed with relief as it coasted down the other side.

4a
2 marks

b) What is special about these metaphors? _____

4b
1 mark

5 a) Write a different simile, metaphor and personification to describe each object.

	Simile	Metaphor	Personification
car			
tower crane			
bag			

5a
9 marks

b) For each of the following objects, write an extended sentence using the metaphor
you created

i) car _____

5b
3 marks

ii) tower crane _____

iii) bag _____

/32

Total for this test

> ## At Level 6 pupils should know that:
> - Alliteration and onomatopoeia both use the sound of words to create effects.
> - Both need to be used sparingly to maintain their impact.

Alliteration

Alliteration is the repetition of a sound, usually at the start of words, for effect. Different letters have different effects. For example:

l and *f* – suggest gentleness and gentle movement
> *The long river lounged lazily along.*

s – can give the effect of softness or sound sinister
> *The spy stared, slyly sniggering.*

b, *d*, *g* – are explosives and can suggest harsher types of movement and aggression
> *He greedily grabbed the grapes.*

Onomatopoeia

Onomatopoeia is the use of words that sound like the noise they name. Some are obvious, such as knock, crunch, hiss, sizzle, whisper, pop, bang and crash, whilst others are more subtle, such as flutter, mumble and rustle.

In the classroom

Activity 1 – alliteration

> Ask pupils to repeat letter sounds and consider what the sound is evocative of (e.g. bbbbb – bubbles; fffff – fluffy, fluttering; hhhhh – laughter; ddddd – sharp, staccato drilling).

> Pick one letter sound and an image (e.g. *d* and a drill). Ask pupils to find words that begin with or feature the sound and that can also be used to portray the image. Use the words to build an alliterative sentence. For example:
> > *The drill dug down, deafening with a deep, dark, dank, dismal drone.*

> Repeat with other sounds.

> Ask pupils to work in pairs to compose lines for an alliteration poem. Give the pairs a common theme and sound. Put the lines from different pairs in different orders and discuss the effect.

> Edit the work together to produce a completed poem.

Activity 2 – onomatopoeia

> Use pupil knowledge and dictionaries to build an onomatopoeia word wall.

> Try different words in sentences, striving to create the most effective.

Sample answers (answers will vary)

1. a) ding-dong b) crunch c) rustle d) sniff
2. a) a word that sounds like what it is naming b) to create an audio effect of what is happening in the text
3. a) 'Peter poked and prodded persistently'; the *p* sound mimics the action of the poking. b) 'Max mostly mumbled and murmured, mouthing meaningless'; the repeated *m* sound is like somebody muttering. c) 'Chugging cheerfully, changing'; the *ch* sounds are like the sounds a steam train makes. d) 'fluttered and floated freely, flitting from flower to flower'; the *f* sound is like the gentle movement of the butterfly.
4. 1 mark for alliteration, 1 mark for effectiveness each question.
   a) The duck glided gracefully, gazing greedily at my bag. b) The player pounded, pouncing proudly on the keys to produce the loud and lively piano music. c) The leaves in the tree rustled and rattled relentlessly, resisting the rough efforts of the wind to remove them. d) The girl laughed with a high, happy, hopeful heart. e) With a whoosh the aeroplane whizzed wickedly, whirring wildly through the sky.

1 Give onomatopoeic words for these sounds:

a) doorbell sound _____   b) footsteps on gravel _____

c) paper moving _____ d) breathing in heavily through your nose _____

	1
4 marks	

2 a) What is onomatopoeia? _____

b) Why might a writer use onomatopoeia? _____

_____

	2
2 marks	

3 In these sentences, underline the examples of alliteration and explain why the writer has used it.

a) Peter poked and prodded persistently until Amir hit him.

The writer used this alliteration to _____

_____

b) Max mostly mumbled and murmured, mouthing meaningless rubbish.

The writer used this alliteration to _____

_____

c) Chugging cheerfully, changing tracks, the train departed.

The writer used this alliteration to _____

_____

d) The butterfly fluttered and floated freely, flitting from flower to flower.

The writer used this alliteration to _____

_____

	3
4 marks	

4 Write a sentence about each of these subjects, using effective alliteration.

a) duck _____

_____

b) piano _____

_____

c) tree _____

_____

d) laughing girl _____

_____

e) aeroplane _____

_____

	4
10 marks	

/20
Total for this test

Creating convincing characters

Convincing characters need some of the following points:

- some description of how they look
- a balance of good and bad points
- information about how they feel and think
- some dialogue to show how they speak
- some dialogue that reveals what others think about them
- insight into how they behave towards others through current or past actions.

Character overviews

These can be summarised in a table:

Name	Appearance	Dialogue	Action	Thoughts	Feelings
Goldilocks	Girl with long, blonde hair	'It's too hot.'	Enters house uninvited; uses, eats and breaks things	What she wants	No remorse, just wants to satisfy her needs

Summary: this character is selfish and unthinking. She doesn't wonder who things belongs to or if they need them. She just takes what she wants.

In the classroom

Look at well-known characters familiar to pupils. Discuss what they know about each character and how they know it.

Complete a character overview table for each character. Evidence can be gathered from memory or (preferably) from a text.

Write a summary for each character.

Give pupils a text containing information about an unfamiliar character and ask them to write a summary of the character. Encourage them to use a table. Discuss responses.

Give pupils an outline of a character they need to create and allow them to work in pairs to discuss and fill in the table to show how they will display the characteristics.

Compare responses and discuss.

Sample answers (answers will vary)

1. 1 mark for good use of material, 1 mark for appropriate and convincing style.
   a) Wolf is a large, fierce animal who is a danger to any creature he meets. His big eyes and teeth are clear signs that he is always on the lookout for his next meal. His famous line, 'All the better to eat you with', is the last most victims ever hear.
   b) Andy is an exceptional man, who loves to help athletes of all abilities reach their full potential. He gives his time and expertise freely and has a genuine interest in people.

2. a)

Name	Appearance	Dialogue	Action	Thoughts	Feelings
Peter	a deceptive smile, dark	'You smell!'	pinches, hides things, lies	I'm better than they are.	smug
Thumper	grey, strong, bright face	'What's that?'	runs, looks into everything	Why? Why?	Wow, fun, interesting,
Exon	blue, 3 legs, enormous	'rgf3£ g^'ln'	puts humans in jars	What odd creatures.	Fascination, curiosity

   b) 1 mark for good use of material, 1 mark for opinions supported.
   Exon is fascinated by the peculiar creatures known as Earthlings. By observing them in his collecting jars he is hoping to learn more about what they do and why. He hopes to gain credibility as an explorer by discovering whether they have intelligence.

1   a) Summarise these characters:

Name	Appearance	Dialogue	Action	Thoughts	Feelings
Wolf	large, fierce, big teeth and eyes, grey fur	'All the better to eat you with.'	plays games with victims before killing them	what to eat next, how to get it	glad to have found dinner

_____

_____

_____

	1a
	2 marks

b)

Name	Appearance	Dialogue	Action	Thoughts	Feelings
Andy	tall, skinny, strong muscles	'I'll teach you – it's easy.'	gives up time to coach children	There might be a good athlete. Everyone deserves a chance.	Glad to help, interested in people

_____

_____

_____

	1b
	2 marks

2   a) Fill in the character table for these characters:

Name	Appearance	Dialogue	Action	Thoughts	Feelings
Peter (a mean little boy)					
Thumper (an inquisitive rabbit)					
Exon (an alien visiting Earth)					

	2a
	15 marks

b) Choose one of the characters and write a description using the information in the table.

_____

_____

_____

_____

_____

	2b
	2 marks

	/21
	Total for this test

Parenthesis

Both brackets and dashes can be used instead of commas to show comments in parenthesis. They are often used in this way if a sentence already contains commas for other purposes:

> *The man, the boy (who was really cross), the girl and the old lady all walked away.*

> *The man, the boy – who was really cross – the girl and the old lady all walked away.*

Brackets

a) Brackets are used to give stage directions about how to speak in play-scripts:

> *Andy: (anxiously) Are you alright?*

b) Brackets are used to allow the writer to speak directly to the reader in an aside:

> *I hate going to the supermarket (and I bet you do too).*

Dashes

Dashes can be used to indicate a slightly longer pause than a comma. This can build tension or indicate comic timing:

> *The man looked around furtively, reached into his coat – and pulled out a knife.*
> *She triumphantly heaved herself onto the airbed, balanced momentarily – and promptly fell into the water!*

In the classroom

Activity 1 – play-scripts

Together, edit a short play-script, putting in performance directions for each speaker. Pupils then perform the script.

Repeat the exercise in pairs, with different directions and / or different play-scripts.

Activity 2 – parenthesis

Ask pupils to write a sentence with a comment in parenthesis punctuated with commas.

Ask them to rewrite their sentences using brackets and then again with dashes. In partners, pupils then discuss the difference.

Collect responses and then emphasise that there is no difference. It is a matter of clarity (where commas are already used in a sentence) and personal preference.

Activity 3 – tension and comic timing

Ask pupils to complete a sentence such as *The car slowed, the window slid open – …*

Collect and compare responses, sorting them into tension and comic sentences.

Sample answers (answers will vary)

1.

	Parenthesis	Comic timing	Dramatic effect
a) He lifted the lid – and out popped the mouse!		✓	possibly
b) The team – which was by far the best – raced to victory.	✓		
c) The man raised his arm – and fired.			✓
d) They were laughing at someone – me!		✓	possibly
e) Ian slipped on the wet patch – and fell over!		✓	possibly
f) Some people – who are rather silly – use too many dashes in their writing.	✓		

2.

	Parenthesis	Comment to the reader	Stage direction
a) My sister laughed (like the mean person we know she is).		✓	
b) Han: (crossly) Go away!			✓
c) The table (which had a broken leg) collapsed.	✓		
d) The man (who was really fat) had to buy two seats on the plane.	✓		
e) Nye: (whispering) Look over there.			✓
f) They were so wrong (just like you were).		✓	

3. a) which had a puncture b) whilst we were unpacking c) although it was brand new d) who always looked so perfect

4. a) The fish, dog, hamster and cat (who all hated the rat) turned away. b) I went (although I would rather have pulled my hair out) to keep the peace – as you would have. c) If we raise money – and we could – then it would be better, especially given the difficulties, to get the support of the staff first. d) If – and this is a big if – I decide to take you (which is not certain at this time) then you would need to change your attitude, which is totally unacceptable, and apologise to Olivia.

5. a) but he wasn't as good as you b) you know the sort c) and we know why d) not like you

1 Complete the table to show how the dashes are used.

	Parenthesis	Comic timing	Dramatic effect
a) He lifted the lid – and out popped the mouse!			
b) The team – which was by far the best – raced to victory.			
c) The man raised his arm – and fired.			
d) They were laughing at someone – me!			
e) Ian slipped on the wet patch – and fell over!			
f) Some people – who are rather silly – use too many dashes in their writing.			

1 | 6 marks

2 Complete the table to show how the brackets are used.

	Parenthesis	Comment to the reader	Stage direction
a) My sister laughed (like the mean person we know she is).			
b) Han: (crossly) Go away!			
c) The table (which had a broken leg) collapsed.			
d) The man (who was really fat) had to buy two seats on the plane.			
e) Nye: (whispering) Look over there.			
f) They were so wrong (just like you were).			

2 | 6 marks

3 Mark the parentheses with brackets or dashes.

a) The bike which had a puncture skidded across the road.

b) The dog whilst we were unpacking escaped and ran away.

c) The bus although it was brand new had a broken sat-nav system.

d) The girl who always looked so perfect was staring straight at me.

3 | 4 marks

4 Use commas, brackets and dashes to punctuate these sentences so they are clear.

a) The fish dog hamster and cat who all hated the rat turned away.

b) I went although I would rather have pulled my hair out to keep the peace as you would have.

c) If we raise money and we could then it would be better especially given the difficulties to get the support of the staff first.

d) If and this is a big if I decide to take you which is not certain at this time then you would need to change your attitude which is totally unacceptable and apologise to Olivia.

4 | 4 marks

5 Write an aside to the reader in each pair of brackets.

a) He thought he was good at football (_____).

b) She was one of those girls (_____) who always knows everything.

c) They said I should go (_____).

d) She was a really frightening teacher (_____).

5 | 4 marks

/24

Total for this test

Colons

- If a quotation is longer than a few words, then it can be introduced with a colon:

  As Judge Berry said: 'Do not underestimate the magnitude of the problem.'

- Before a colon that introduces lists, further information and explanations, there must be a full sentence:

  For holidays I pack few clothes: a pair of shorts, two tops and sandals.

Semi-colons

- Semi-colons give writing greater precision. They are halfway between a full stop and a comma:

  The English tutor was tall and strict; the French master was short and funny.

- Semi-colons separate items in a list where commas are being used for other purposes in the list:

  In the club were Andy, who was a fantastic coach; Obi, who was a real encouragement to everyone; Max, who pushed us all to try hard; and, last but not least, Eleanor, who made sure we had fun.

In the classroom

Give pupils sets of independent clauses (simple sentences) that can be paired in content through contrast or more information / explanation. There may be more than one possible pairing for each clause.

Ask pupils to work with a partner and pair the sentences as they think best (so answers may vary).

Discuss the pairings and decide whether they explain or give further information (make one pile of these) or make a contrast (put these in another pile).

Explain that pairs that develop the information through explanation or further information can be written as one sentence with a colon between, and that those that contrast can be written as one sentence with a semi-colon between. Emphasise that a capital letter is not used after the colon or semi-colon unless there is a proper noun.

Ask pupils to write the sentences with the correct punctuation.

Sample answers (answers will vary)

1. 1 mark for correct punctuation, 1 mark for explanation.
   a) ; contrasting sentences b) : further information c) : list and further information d) ; contrasting sentences e) : explanation

2. introduce lists, introduce quotations, introduce explanations / additional information

3. separate items on lists where comma is already used, separate contrasting sentences

4. a) I put lots of vegetables in the casserole b) William, who hated them; Tom, who started the club; and Lucy. c) the boy was short and plump. d) he needed to eat more. e) running, swimming and football. f) we enjoyed lots of different books. g) The gardens were warm and welcoming h) I could understand her unease i) it had been a tiring day. j) I tossed and turned all night. k) it was too loud and out of tune. j) Stephanie loved it.

1 Punctuate these sentences correctly using either a colon or a semi-colon. After each, explain your answer.

a) James was a tall elite athlete _____ Olivia was a short gifted academic.

Reason: _____

b) James was a tall elite athlete _____ he captained the basketball team.

Reason: _____

c) James was a tall elite athlete _____ running, swimming and cycling were his strengths.

Reason: _____

d) James was a tall elite athlete _____ Joshua was a strong talented farmer.

Reason: _____

e) James was a tall elite athlete _____ he had trained for years.

Reason: _____

	1
	10 marks

2 Give three uses of the colon in sentence writing.

a) _____

b) _____

c) _____

	2
	3 marks

3 Give two uses of the semi-colon in sentence writing.

a) _____

b) _____

	3
	2 marks

4 Complete these sentences so the punctuation is correct.

a) _____ : carrots, potatoes, onions and peas.

b) In our group were Caitlin, who loved eco activities; _____

_____

c) The man was tall and skinny; _____

_____

d) The man was tall and skinny: _____

_____

e) He enjoyed lots of different sports: _____

_____

f) He enjoyed lots of different sports; _____

_____

	4
	12 marks

g) _____ ; the castle was tall and forbidding.

h) _____ : the castle was tall and forbidding.

i) He fell asleep instantly: _____

_____

j) He fell asleep instantly; _____

_____

k) William was irritated by the music: _____

_____

l) William was irritated by the music; _____

_____

	/27
	Total for this test

> **At Level 6 pupils should know that:**
> - Correct speech punctuation is essential.
> - Speech style should be appropriate for each individual character.
> - Apostrophes should be used correctly for omission and possession.

Speech

Direct speech rules:

- Capital letters start speech sentences
- New speaker, new line
- Punctuation or a new line before every speech mark
- Inverted commas around the spoken words

Indirect (reported) speech rules:

- Usually in the past tense and often use 'that'
- No inverted commas around the spoken words:
    He said that he was sorry.

Script writing rules:

- Write the speaker's name, a colon, directions in brackets and then the words to be spoken:
    Nye: (desperately) *You've got to help.*

Apostrophes

For omission to show where letters are omitted in a word. For example: *can't, she'll.*

For possession to show that something belongs to someone:

- Singular nouns add *'s*. For example: *the dog's bone.*
- Singular nouns ending in *s* add *'s* or just *'*. For example:
    James's turn or *James' turn.*
- Plural nouns ending in *s* just add *'*. For example:
    the boys' entrance.
- Plural nouns not ending in *s* add *'s*. For example:
    the children's toys.

Note: Even if the name of the possession is omitted, the apostrophe is still needed. For example:

  It is John's (whistle). I'm going to the doctor's (surgery).

In the classroom

Activity 1 – writing speech

> Play a short recorded conversation between two people.

> Give pupils transcripts of what was said without any indication of who was speaking or speech marks. Listen to the recording again, asking pupils to annotate how the words are said.

> Write the conversation as direct speech, then reported speech, then a play-script. Revise the rules as necessary.

Activity 2 – apostrophes

> Revise the use of apostrophes.

> Give the children words ending in s and ask them to try and use each one in a sentence where an apostrophe is necessary and another sentence where it isn't – or one sentence that uses both. For example:
>
>   *The **car's** engine overheated when we tried to overtake the other **cars**.*

Sample answers (answers will vary)

1. a) it's, its b) Who's, whose c) they're, there, their d) you're, your
2. 1 mark for each apostrophe with a correct reason.
    a) Olivia's (P) wasn't (O) Eleanor's (P) b) Caitlin's (P) mum's (P) can't (O) baker's (P) c) doctor's (P) weren't (O) Jake's (P) d) girls' (P) there'll (O) e) Let's (O) John's (P) mum's (O) f) don't (O) it's (O) Nye's (P) g) wasn't (O)
3. a) 1 mark for each line of dialogue punctuated correctly.
    'Well,' said Gill angrily, 'I don't think it's fair that he gets to go.'
      'Why not?' asked Cleo curiously.
      'Because,' declared Gill, 'he was really badly behaved yesterday.'
      'In that case,' responded Cleo firmly, 'George can go instead.'
    b) 4 marks if correct, 2 marks for a good effort. Gill said that it wasn't fair he got to go. When Cleo asked why, she said he had behaved really badly the day before, so Cleo said that George could go instead.
    c) 1 mark for each line of play-script. Gill: (*angrily*) Well, I don't think it's fair that he gets to go.
    Cleo: (*curiously*) Why not? Gill: Because he was really badly behaved yesterday.
    Cleo: (*firmly*) In that case George can go instead.

1 Choose the correct words to complete these sentences.

a) If _____ alright with you, we can finish _____ decoration tomorrow. (its / it's)

b) _____ going to decide _____ turn it is to wash up? (who's / whose)

c) If _____ going _____ then _____ mum should be told.
(there / they're / their)

d) When _____ near, phone us on _____ mobile. (you're / your)

1

9 marks

2 Put apostrophes where they are needed in these sentences. Write the reason for each apostrophe.

a) Olivias home wasnt far from Eleanors.

Reason: _____

b) If Caitlins mums car has a puncture then we cant go to the bakers.

Reason: _____

c) At the doctors, we werent allowed to eat Jakes sweets.

Reason: _____

d) If the boys take the girls ball therell be a fight!

Reason: _____

e) Lets go to Johns and see if his mums made any cakes.

Reason: _____

f) Dont forget that its today that the books need to go back to Nyes.

Reason: _____

g) The dog saw its lead and thought its owner wasnt going to take it out.

Reason: _____

2

19 marks

3 Read this text.

> Well said Gill angrily, I don't think it's fair that he gets to go. Why not asked Cleo curiously.
>
> Because, declared Gill, he was really badly behaved yesterday. In that case responded Cleo firmly, George can go instead.

a) Write the text correctly as direct speech.

_____
_____
_____

3a

4 marks

b) Change the conversation to reported speech.

_____
_____
_____

3b

4 marks

c) Write the conversation as a play-script.

_____
_____
_____
_____

3c

4 marks

/40

Total for this test

> ## At Level 6 pupils should know that:
> - In writing, the spelling of the majority of words, including more difficult words, should be correct.

Supporting spelling

For Level 6, it is expected that pupils will spell the vast majority of words correctly. At this stage, teaching to address spelling weaknesses probably needs to be tailored to individual pupil need. A knowledge of harder letter strings, prefixes, suffixes, word families and an understanding of etymology will all support more accurate spelling.

Harder letter strings

The letter strings each pupil finds difficult will vary, but common problems are with –tious, –cious, –ance, –ence, –able, –ible and –ough.

Prefixes and suffixes

Knowing prefixes and suffixes and their meanings helps in building multisyllabic words, especially where sounds change (think how spelling *music* could help with spelling *musician*).

Word families

These are words that can be grouped in a particular way, perhaps through a spelling pattern (*bough, though, thorough*), meaning (*rubbish, detritus, residue*) or by the inclusion of a particular root word (*science, scientist, scientific, conscience*).

Etymology

Etymology is the study of word origins and how they have changed over time.

In the classroom

Give pupils a piece of their own work with spelling errors indicated but not corrected.

↓

Ask them to list the spellings (preferably in a separate spelling notebook) and have another attempt at spelling them.

↓

Allow pupils to use dictionaries to check their revised spelling and correct as necessary.

↓

Ask pupils to group the corrected words in any way they can.

↓

Establish if there are any patterns in the errors. If so, create a page in the notebook dedicated to this group of words that pupils can add to over time and refer to when working on spellings.

Sample answers (answers will vary)

1. 1 mark for each correct row.

Word	Meaning	Country of origin
a) sampan	boat	China
b) avocado	fruit	Spain
c) graffiti	marks and writings on buildings and paths	Italy

3. 1 mark for three correct words in a box, 2 marks for five.
a) illegal, legality, legalise, legalese, illegally b) special, partial, spatial, crucial, martial c) notes, rhythm, beat, melody, instrument d) ridicule, taunting, scorn, derision, farce e) commitment, committee, committed, noncommittal, committal f) biology, biography, microbiology, autobiography, biodiversity g) pretentious, contentious, ambitious, cautiously, expeditious h) referee, referral, reference, deferred, deferential i) irregular, sporadic, variable, anomalous, bizarre

2. 1 mark for each box completed correctly.

Word	Country of origin	Meaning	Two related words (if possible)
daisy	day's eye (open dawn till dusk)	Old English	no related words
phobia	fear / horror	Greek	agoraphobia, claustrophobia, arachnophobia, hydrophobia
credit	worthy of belief	Latin	creditable, creditability, incredible
circumference	around (the edge)	Latin	circumnavigate, circumstantial, circumstances
mania	great enthusiasm or madness	Greek	kleptomania, megalomania, egomania, maniac
graph	write	Greek	graphic, photography, autograph, telegraph

1 Use a dictionary to give the meanings of these words and their country of origin.

Word	Meaning	Country of origin
a) sampan		
b) avocado		
c) graffiti		

1

3 marks

2 Use a dictionary to complete the table showing the etymology of these words.

Word	Country of origin	Meaning	Two related words (if possible)
daisy			
phobia			
credit			
circumference			
mania			
graph			

2

18 marks

3 Complete this table of word families by finding (and spelling correctly) at least five words for each box.

a) Words using the root word *legal*	b) Words ending in the letter string *–ial*	c) Words related in meaning to *music*
d) Synonyms of *mockery*	e) Words using the root word *commit*	f) Words with the prefix *bio–*
g) Words containing in the letter string *–tious*	h) Words using the root word *refer*	i) Antonyms of *regular*

3

18 marks

/39

Total for this test

Race report

Connie Preece stunned the crowd at Basin Bash Triathlon this weekend. She beat fierce competition to become the new course champion. After leading the swim, Connie was the first out of the water and was through transition 1 before the next competitor, Jo Baker, had reached the exit ramp.

Disaster struck on the bike, where Connie suffered a puncture after 15 km and lost precious minutes fixing it. Jo and three other competitors raced past, determined to make the most of this unexpected boon. Once she was mounted again, Connie strained every muscle to bridge the gap with the lead cyclists, achieving this just before the last lap. The group went around the last lap more or less together, with Jo leading the way into transition 2 and Connie in 4th place, just 22 seconds behind.

Bikes racked and helmets off, the final race started. Connie steadily moved forward, gaining on Jo. At the half-way mark they were neck-and-neck, with a group just yards behind. It was down to mental strength and staying power and Connie proved her mettle. With an incredible spurt of power, she began to pull ahead. The group tried to stay with her, but their effort on the bike was taking its toll. Connie sprinted on to victory and a new course record.

Triathlon

Triathlon is an exciting sport that is growing in popularity among adults and children.

Imagine waking up and deciding to go for a swim. In open water (like a lake). Oh, and lets make that a kilometre or so, with no pool edges to grab onto every 25 m.

What should we do next?

Perhaps a bike ride – the odd 40 km should be enough because then we could run.

How does 10 km sound to you? Really? It sounds like hard work?

That's because it is. Hard work, but enormous fun in a sport that gets your adrenalin pumping and challenges you to find your limits.

FORGET THE GYM – THIS IS FITNESS IN THE REAL WORLD

Triathlon is for you!

Triathlons, as the name suggests, involve three disciplines: swim, bike and run. Whatever your age, ability or experience, there is a race for you. You race against the clock with transitions between the disciplines timed as well.

Race distances vary, depending on the race type.

Race type	Swim	Bike	Run
Sprint	750 m (or 400 m in a pool)	20 km	5 km
Olympic	1.5 km	40 km	10 km
70.3	1.9 km	90 km	21 km
Ironman	3.8 km	180 km	42 km

My first triathlon

I arrived at the venue before anyone's alarm should be going off (early starts are the blight of the triathlon world). I racked my rather ordinary looking bike next to some serious speed machines, laid out my shoes and other equipment and nervously donned a wet suit for the swim.

Swim hat and goggles in hand, I arrived at the swim start as the sun peeped over the horizon, curious to see the cause of the commotion. With minutes to go, we were herded into the water – a perfect wake-up system as cold water leaked through the zip and shocked my nerves into a violent protest. Milling around and exchanging nervous smiles, my compatriots and I tried to see the buoys we would be swimming towards.

The horn sounded and the water became a churning mass of flailing arms and legs. Battered and kicked, I struggled to breathe and pushed my arms like

windmills to break free of my assailants. Once in clear water, I checked for the buoy, which had disappeared. A quick check showed I was swimming back the way I had come! A quick turn and off again. And then again. And again. And again. My lungs burned and I felt a desperate need to get out of the water, escape from the never-ending toil.

Swim finished, I ran on numbed feet only to realise I didn't know which of those rows of bikes held mine. There – I stumbled towards the bike. Peeling down my wet suit, I rammed my helmet on, slipped uncooperative feet into bike shoes and put on my cycle jersey. Which adhered to my wet arms and refused to budge. Fighting through, precious seconds … minutes … ticked by before I, well, *tried* to sprint for the bike exit. It was actually more like a wobbly jog.

At the mount line, I pushed off and started pedalling. As I flew past other riders I felt a moment of sheer exhilaration. Wow! Maybe these people could swim but they sure couldn't cycle. 10 km later it was

a grim fight to push the pedals around, pull up, push down, pull up, push down. Unwilling to relinquish the time I had gained I fought around the course. Up hills

– surely there should be a downhill somewhere? So intent, I almost missed the turn into the next transition, swerving wildly at the last moment as a marshal frantically signalled.

Off the bike. Run. Rack the bike. Helmet. Run. Shoes on. And off I went again. Sort of.

Now my legs seemed to realise that there was something going on and were sending messages of, 'What's happening?' to my brain. 'Why do I have to keep doing this? What about a walk? Aw, come on!' Only the pressure of the spectators kept my legs turning long after my weak-willed body would have quit. A water station – I gratefully grabbed a drink as I passed, only to have it splash out of the cup straight into my face before I even got a mouthful. A new form of water torture. Tiny slopes became mountains to conquer and I knew I couldn't go another step. But I did – another, another, another. Until there it was –   the finish.

Suddenly, I felt a surge of strength course through my limbs and, pasting on an enormous smile for the waiting camera, I sprinted towards the line, arms aloft as I went beneath the gantry.

Collapsing to the floor, I wanted to start all over again. Now! I needed to do all those things right. The bug had bitten!

Reading assessment questions

You have 1 hour to complete this assessment

Questions on 'My first triathlon'

1 The writer says: 'the sun peeped over the horizon, curious to see the cause of the commotion'. What does the image mean and why is it effective?

_____

_____

_____

_____

_____

_____

	1
2 marks

2 Before the start of the swim race, the writer calls his companions 'compatriots'. When the race starts, they become 'assailants'. Explain this apparent contradiction.

_____

_____

_____

_____

_____

_____

	2
3 marks

3 The writer uses repetition several times. Explain the effects of these repeated phrases. Support your answer with references to the text.

_____

_____

_____

_____

_____

	3
2 marks

4 'Off the bike. Run. Rack the bike. Helmet. Run shoes on.' What effect is the writing trying to create with these very short sentences?

_____

_____

_____

_____

_____

_____

	3
3 marks

(5) 'Precious seconds … minutes … ticked by.' Why does the writer use ellipses in this sentence?

_____

_____

_____

_____

	5
	2 marks

(6) Were you surprised when the writer wanted to do the race again straight after the finish? Explain your answer with references to the text.

_____

_____

_____

_____

_____

_____

_____

	6
	3 marks

(7) Explain the phrase at the end of the article: 'The bug had bitten.'

_____

_____

_____

_____

	7
	1 mark

(8) What were the things that happened that the writer wanted to go back and get right?

_____

_____

_____

_____

_____

_____

	8
	2 marks

(9) From the advert for the Scarab Triathlon Club, explain the effectiveness of the phrase: 'Support and encouragement with every stroke and step you take.'

_____

_____

_____

_____

_____

_____

	9
	2 marks

Questions on 'Race report'

10 From its context in the report, what do you think is the meaning of the phrase 'bridge the gap'?

_____

_____

	10
2 marks

11 How does the writer convey this was a very close-run race? Refer to the text in your answer.

_____

_____

_____

_____

_____

_____

	11
2 marks

12 What does the writer mean by Connie 'proved her mettle'?

_____

_____

_____

	12
1 mark

13 How does the writer's choice of words and phrases convey the excitement and tension of the race? Refer to the text to support your answer.

_____

_____

_____

_____

_____

_____

_____

	13
3 marks

Questions on introductory page

14 Read the section starting with '**Imagine** …'
What techniques does the writer use to involve the reader and draw a response? Refer to the text in your answer.

_____

_____

_____

_____

_____

_____

	14
3 marks

15 How does the writer convey that triathlon is suitable for anyone?

_____

_____

_____

_____

	15
	3 marks

16 What is effective about the presentation of the information on race types?

_____

_____

_____

	16
	1 mark

Questions on the whole booklet

17 Based on the booklet, what is your opinion of triathlon? Justify your answer by references to the text.

_____

_____

_____

_____

_____

_____

_____

_____

_____

	17
	3 marks

18 What do you think the author was trying to achieve by writing this booklet? Give three purposes and evidence to support your answers.

Purpose 1 _____

_____

_____

Purpose 2 _____

_____

_____

Purpose 3 _____

_____

_____

	18
	6 marks

	/44
	Total for this assessment

Below are some different writing tasks. Your teacher will tell you which task to complete.
You have 40 minutes to complete this writing task.

PLEASE SIR

As secretary of the School Council, you are asked to write to the Chair of Governors.

You are trying to persuade him to buy the piece of land adjacent to the school as a playing field. The school doesn't have any proper sports facilities at the moment.

Use techniques that will persuade him that this is a good idea.

Reasons to buy the field

1.

2.

3.

4.

5.

Persuasion techniques

1.

2.

3.

4.

5.

You have 40 minutes to complete this writing task.

BEWILDERED BY BULLYING

Write a diary entry about being drawn into bullying at school.

The group of friends you hang around with have started picking on someone. You haven't joined in but haven't stuck up for the victim either.

Reflect on your feelings and discuss the courses of action that are open to you.

Use this spider diagram to help plan your diary entry.

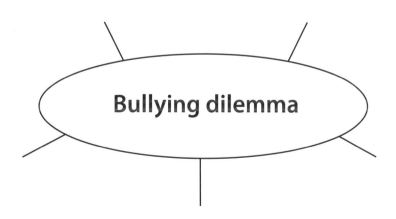

You have 40 minutes to complete this writing task.

THE GHOST STORY

Write the opening to a ghost story. You need to set the scene and introduce two characters.

Think about creating the atmosphere and making your characters believable.

Use techniques that will create tension in the opening.

Remember, you are not writing the full story.

Use this boxes to help you plan your opening.

I will create tension with:	Character 1

Setting	Character 2

You have 40 minutes to complete this writing task.

HOLIDAY HULLABALOO

Write a letter to a friend about a disastrous family holiday.

Think about what went wrong on the holiday and why.

Remember to include your own and other people's reactions and feelings.

You have 40 minutes to complete this writing task.

TOO MANY COOKS SPOIL THE BROTH

This proverb means that if too many people try to do something, they end up ruining it.

Write a short story to illustrate this proverb.

Reading assessment answers

Questions on 'My first triathlon'

1. 1 mark for each point with an explanation, to a maximum of two points, or 2 marks for very well explained two points. Personification; the sun rise is like someone peeping over the horizon. It can see because it is providing the light. The writer suggests that the sun is curious to see what was going on, just like a person would be.

2. 1 mark for each point with an explanation, to a maximum of three points.
Before the race they are sharing an experience together, like friends, 'exchanging nervous smiles' and making comments to each other; after the start they become opponents, competitors racing against each other; in the rush to get started there are 'flailing arms and legs' and people get 'battered and kicked' so it is like being attacked and they are the people attacking you ('assailants').

3. 1 mark for each point with an explanation, to a maximum of two points, or 2 marks for very well explained one point. In the swim it says 'again. And then again. And again. And again.' On the bike it was 'pull up, push down, pull up, push down' and in the run it was 'another, another, another'. This shows that in each part of the race, the effort had to be kept up and seemed to be going on for a long time, so the movements became mechanical and rhythmic.

4. 1 mark for each point with an explanation, to a maximum of three points, or 3 marks for very well explained two points. They are imperative so it is like someone shouting orders that have to be obeyed. It is also like a list that the racer is checking off to make sure everything gets done. The fast pace of the short sentences shows that this is a busy part of the race, with lots of different little things to be done very quickly.

5. 1 mark for each point with an explanation to a maximum of two points.
To show that time was passing and being wasted; the racer was impatient to get on but couldn't; precious time was being wasted.

6. 1 mark for each point with an explanation, to a maximum of three points.
EITHER Yes (Only seemed to enjoy the first part of the bike, got battered in the swim and kept going the wrong way and wanted to 'escape', feet were numb afterwards and could only do a 'wobbly jog', then the bike became a 'grim fight'; wanted to stop on the run – the questions and the 'weak-willed body', plus the 'water torture' with the water.

   OR No (The description is all full of energy and even though it was hard the racer never gave up but kept pushing on and trying to go as fast as possible 'pushed my arms like windmills … tried to sprint … so intent, I almost missed the turn'; felt 'exhilaration' on the bike course 'Wow' and at the end had a 'surge of energy … smile … sprinted … arms aloft').

7. The racer is hooked into doing the triathlon and will want to keep doing it.

8. 1 mark for two points, 2 marks for three points.
Wrong direction in the swim (more than once); not knowing where bike was; putting on a jersey that stuck to wet arms; throwing water in face.

9. 'Every stroke and step' refers to all the swimming and running you will do (1 mark). 'Every step' is also on your triathlon journey and helping you learn how to do it better (1 mark).

Questions on 'Race report'

10. Catch up with the people who are in front.

11. 1 mark for each point with an explanation, up to 2 marks.
    The writer says 'fierce competition', 'bridge the gap', the last lap of the bike they were 'more or less together' and then we are told Connie is just seconds behind. Half way on the run they are 'neck and neck' and the race was just down to 'mental strength' so all through they are close and it wasn't certain till the end who would win.

12. She showed what she was made of; she showed that she was a strong person (physically and mentally).

13. 1 mark for each point with an explanation, to a maximum of three points, or 3 marks for very well explained two points.
    The crowd were 'stunned' so the audience had an extreme reaction; choice of strong emotive words such as 'fierce', 'incredible' and 'victory' build an atmosphere that is exciting; the 'disaster struck' and 'precious minutes' show the importance to the competitors, to the others it was a 'boon'; the writer shows how the athletes are so close together and how first one leads and then the other, which shows the tension at the time.

Questions on the introductory page

14. 1 point for each point made and explained, up to 3.
    The writer asks the reader to put themselves in the position which makes them think what it would be like; the style is very chatty and informal (words such as 'oh', 'perhaps', 'really') so it is as if the writer is just talking to the reader; addressing the reader as 'you' makes it personal and the use of 'we' makes it sound like the writer and reader are in it together; questions invite a response because the reader automatically answers them; the questions follow on as if the writer is listening to the reader's response and having a conversation.

15. 1 point for each point made and explained, up to 2.
    It says popular with 'adults and children', the poster states that 'Triathlon is for you', it says 'whatever age, ability or experience' and shows that there are shorter races too.

16. In a table so easy to read and compare the different race distances.

Questions on the whole booklet

17. 1 point for each point made and explained, up to 3.
    Either FOR (Introduction says it's 'an exciting sport', 'growing popularity', 'enormous fun', a good way to keep fit, 'challenges you' suitable for everyone; first race says 'exhilaration' on the bike, 'surge of energy' at end, wanted to do it again; exciting race in 'Race report', good to watch as well as 'stunned the crowd'; advert sayscan get support and help in clubs.

    Or AGAINST (Introduction says 'sounds like hard work? That's because it is'; really early starts 'before anyone's alarm'; expensive equipment 'serious speed machines', 'cold water ... numbed feet', swimming in a 'churning mass', bike seems all uphill – 'there should be a downhill', legs not wanting to run, 'water torture' when can't get a drink. Race report shows problems whilst racing – 'disaster' of puncture, level of effort 'strained every muscle', 'effort ... taking its toll').

18. 1 mark for identifying purpose, 1 mark for showing evidence for each part.
    Information – tells about what happens in a race in the Report and First triathlon account; race distances in the table.
    Entertainment – first section with the imagination section; account of first race and what went wrong.
    Persuasion – to make people want to try triathlon (poster, showing everyone starts somewhere and it's OK if things go wrong).

Marking Level 6 writing

When you are marking the test piece of writing (or any other writing) at Level 6, these are the elements of writing to consider and the total marks each is worth. The mark a pupil should achieve for **Level 6 overall is a minimum of 15/25.**

AF1 Write imaginative, interesting and thoughtful texts		**Composition and effect** • **Ideas** are thoroughly explored and developed • Writing achieves its intended **purpose** successfully • The **reader's interest** is firmly engaged • A **variety of features** and techniques are used successfully • **Viewpoint** is well focused, developed and maintained • A range of **stylistic features** are used to achieve the purpose **Marks out of 11**
AF2 Produce texts which are appropriate to the task, reader and purpose	* * * * * * * * * * * AF7 Select appropriate and effective vocabulary	
AF3 Organise and present whole texts effectively, sequencing and structuring information, ideas and events		**Text structure and organisation** • Structure is **controlled** • Structure is **suited to the purpose** • Sections / **paragraphs are linked** to signal an overall direction clearly for the reader • Ideas are **well organised** within sections / paragraphs to support the purpose • Purpose is supported with a range of **cohesion devices** **Marks out of 6**
AF4 Construct paragraphs and use cohesion within and between paragraphs		
AF5 Vary sentences for clarity, purpose and effect		**Sentence structure and punctuation** • Generally controlled use of a variety of **simple and complex sentences** • A range of **grammatical structures** are used to vary sentence length and focus • A **range of verb forms** is used and shifts are managed generally well • Mostly secure range of **appropriate punctuation** is used to mark the structure of sentences • Punctuation promotes **clarity** **Marks out of 6**
AF6 Write with technical accuracy of syntax and punctuation in phrases, clauses and sentences	* * * * * * * * * * *	
AF8 Use the correct spelling		**Spelling** • Spelling is generally accurate, including that of irregular words **Marks out of 2**